# When Cupid's Arrow is a Pain in the Ass

**FREEDOM FROM
DESTRUCTIVE RELATIONSHIP SYNDROME**

Steven Heller, Ph.D. has been in private practice since 1969 and has led training seminars for health care professionals based on his innovative approach *"Unconscious Restructuring"* which he says is Hypnosis without Hypnosis." Dr. Heller has presented this program for therapists, hospital staffs, universities, medical and dental personnel and associations.

Dr. Heller wrote *"When Cupid's Arrow is a Pain in the Ass"* (H.I. Enterprises ©1996) based on his extensive experience working with individuals and couples on their relationship issues. He believes that most relationships improve when people have tools that work. "Cupids Arrow" and his new seminar program based on this book, are meant to do just that - give people tools to create happier, more loving and successful relationships.

Dr. Heller resides with his wife Susan in Westlake Village, California and has his offices in Calabasas, CA. He was born in Los Angeles where he has lived most of his life. He earned a law degree from La Salle University and his Ph.D. in Psychology from California Western University.

His first book, "Monsters and Magical Sticks - There's No Such Thing as Hypnosis" (written with Terry Lee Steele, Ph.D.– New Falcon Publications ©1987) set new standards in the practice of hypnotherapy. His students and colleagues gave him the title of "The Wizard" and have presented him with an extensive collection of wizards.

For information about seminar schedules or to order copies of this book please use the request form at the end of this book.

# When Cupid's Arrow is a Pain in the Ass

### FREEDOM FROM DESTRUCTIVE RELATIONSHIP SYNDROME

BY
### STEVEN HELLER, PH.D.

H.I. Enterprises    Thousand Oaks, California

## WHEN CUPID'S ARROW IS A PAIN IN THE ASS
Freedom from Destructive Relationship Syndrome
By Steven Heller, Ph.D.

Copyright © 1996 by Steven Heller, Ph.D.

All rights reserved under the Pan-American and International Copyright Conventions. No parts of this book may be copied or reproduced, in whole or in part, in any form or by any means, electronic or mechanical, including photocopying, recording, or by any information storage and retrieval system now known or hereafter invented, except for brief quotations embodied in critical articles and reviews, without written permission from the author or the publisher. Inquires may be addressed to the publisher:

**H.I. Enterprises
P.O. Box 3604
Thousand Oaks, CA 91359-0604
(800) 806-0407 USA**

Cover design by Hortensia Chu
Printed in the U.S.A. by KNI Incorporated

**Library of Congress Cataloging-Publication Data**
Heller, Steven, 1939-
   When Cupid's Arrow is a Pain in the Ass
   Freedom from Destructive Relationships / by Steven Heller, Ph.D.
     Includes Index
     ISBN 0-9639994-5-1 : $12.95
      1. Interpersonal Relationships    I Title
      2. Marriage
      3. Love
HQ801.H325  1996                                 96-094302
646.7'7                                                       CIP

# Table of Contents

**INTRODUCTION**
Relationship: Thy Name is often Misery .................... 11

**CHAPTER 1:** **Destructive Relationship Syndrome** ............ 19
    Time, Effort and Money ............................... 20
    The Shrinks .......................................... 22
    Not Therapy .......................................... 23
    The First Secret ..................................... 25
    Cathy – Mr. Right? ................................... 26
    Points To Remember ................................... 30

**CHAPTER 2:** **Destructive Relationship Syndrome II** ......... 31
    Definition ........................................... 31
    Robert and Betty – DRS Classic ....................... 32
    Clear Differences .................................... 34
    Foundation Issues .................................... 36
    The Honeymoon and The Disaster ....................... 37
    What about Love at First Sight? ...................... 39
    Points To Remember ................................... 40

**CHAPTER 3:** **In the Beginning** ............................. 41
    A Little Parable ..................................... 41
    Enter the Baby ....................................... 43
    Four Painful Strategies .............................. 43
    The Addictive Family ................................. 46
    Violence ............................................. 46
    Unfinished Business .................................. 48
    Self-Fulfilling Prophecy ............................. 49
    Ending the Beginning ................................. 51
    Points To Remember ................................... 54

**CHAPTER 4:** **DRS in Disguise** .............................. 55
    The Crutch and the Crutchie .......................... 56
    The Savior and the Lost Soul ......................... 58
    Becoming a Savior .................................... 59
    The Therapist and the Patient ........................ 60
    The Teacher and the Pupil ............................ 62
    The Sad Sack ......................................... 63
    On the Rebound ....................................... 64
    The Bully and the Victim ............................. 65
    Wrapping It Up ....................................... 66
    Points To Remember ................................... 68

**CHAPTER 5:** **Just a Little Insanity** ....................... 69
    DRS and Insanity ..................................... 70
    Jim – Rescues the Damsel ............................. 71

| | |
|---|---|
| Recurring Insanity | 72 |
| A Little DRS | 73 |
| More Insanity | 74 |
| Home Work | 76 |
| Linda – the Jerk Finder | 77 |
| Points To Remember | 80 |

**CHAPTER 6:   Instant Love?** .................................. 81
| | |
|---|---|
| The Magic Fades | 82 |
| Instant Attraction | 83 |
| Defining Instant Attraction | 84 |
| Mini-Hallucinations | 86 |
| Two Patterns | 87 |
| Points To Remember | 88 |

**CHAPTER 7:   Warning Patterns** .............................. 89
| | |
|---|---|
| The Twelve Patterns of DRS | 90 |
| Self-Evaluation One | 91 |
| Denial and Avoidance | 93 |
| Herb and Sylvia – The Date | 94 |
| Points To Remember | 98 |

**CHAPTER 8:   DRS or Not** ..................................... 99
| | |
|---|---|
| Too Fast on the Draw | 99 |
| Obsession | 101 |
| Louise – Bewitched and Besotted | 102 |
| Withdrawal Symptoms | 104 |
| Positively Negative | 106 |
| Not Me! | 107 |
| The Anxiety Factor | 108 |
| The Elevator Factor | 109 |
| A General Map | 110 |
| Points To Remember | 112 |

**CHAPTER 9:   What's the Score?** ............................ 113
| | |
|---|---|
| Sally - Scale of Success | 114 |
| Instructions for Scale Two | 115 |
| DRS: Scale Two | 116 |
| DRS Scale Two: Keeping Score | 119 |
| Already Committed | 120 |
| Paula and Alan – Ten Years of Misery | 121 |
| Points To Remember | 124 |

**CHAPTER 10:   The Second Secret** ........................... 125
| | |
|---|---|
| A Question and Answer | 126 |
| Heads or Tails – A Joke | 126 |
| You Must Ask the Right Question! | 128 |
| Don and Beth – The Schism | 130 |

    The Little Escape .................................... 133
    Two Photographs ..................................... 135
    A Little Plea ........................................ 136
    Points To Remember .................................. 138

**CHAPTER 11: The Question of the Year** ................. 139
    History of the Question .............................. 140
    Question of the Year ................................. 141
    Answer to Question of the Year ....................... 143
    Making Nice .......................................... 144
    Sylvia – No Pleasure ................................. 146
    Banking the Positives ................................ 148
    Points To Remember ................................... 149

**CHAPTER 12: The Journey Continues** .................... 151
    A Question of Esteem ................................. 152
    A Car of Your Dreams ................................. 154
    Seeking Levels ....................................... 155
    Finding Dog Poo ...................................... 157
    Three for One ........................................ 159
    A Little Inventory ................................... 161
    Relationship Strategy ................................ 162
    Points To Remember ................................... 164

**CHAPTER 13: Golden Rule Days** ......................... 165
    To Affirm or Not ..................................... 167
    A Little Affirmation Test ............................ 168
    The Blackboard ....................................... 169
    Flash Cards .......................................... 172
    Stage One ............................................ 173
    Stage Two ............................................ 174
    Stage Three .......................................... 174
    Adding it up ......................................... 175
    Points To Remember ................................... 176

**CHAPTER 14: Talk – Talk – Talk** ....................... 177
    Bad Talking .......................................... 178
    The Blamer ........................................... 179
    The Placater ......................................... 181
    The Distracter ....................................... 182
    The Computer ......................................... 183
    Less Talk ............................................ 186
    Straight Talk ........................................ 186
    Points To Remember ................................... 188

**CHAPTER 15: More Talk** ................................ 189
    A Second Question .................................... 189
    Four Steps Communication ............................. 191

Step One .................................................. 191
Step Two .................................................. 194
Step Three ................................................ 197
Warning – Warning ........................................ 198
Step Four ................................................. 198
More Four Steps .......................................... 200
The Little Ones ........................................... 201
The Answer ............................................... 201
Points To Remember ..................................... 203

**CHAPTER 16: Map Making 101** ............................ 205
Expectations ............................................. 206
The Continuing Journey .................................. 207
New Maps ................................................ 208
Low Expectations ........................................ 209
A Map to Follow ......................................... 211
The Map Continues ...................................... 212
Points to Remember ..................................... 215

**CHAPTER 17: Maps To Go** ................................ 217
FB – Self-Absorbed ....................................... 217
Relationship Questions ................................... 220
Your Turn ................................................ 223
I Don't Want To .......................................... 226
Responsibility ............................................ 226
Points to Remember ..................................... 228

**CHAPTER 18: Sculpting Your Map** ........................ 229
Maps For One or Two .................................... 230
The Slob – Attached or Not .............................. 231
Married to a Slob ........................................ 232
Not Attached ............................................. 234
Really Bad Behavior ..................................... 235
Obligations and Duties .................................. 236
Admirable or Not ........................................ 238
Points to Remember ..................................... 240

**CHAPTER 19: Leave Taking** .............................. 241
Best Wart Forward ....................................... 242
Old Wisdom .............................................. 244
Guru or Not? ............................................. 246
Failure ................................................... 248
Epilogue ................................................. 250

**INDEX** .................................................. 251

# Acknowledgments

To my wife Susan, Thank you for all your efforts and contributions. She had the tedious task of reading rough - rough drafts of this work, repeatedly. While she often caused me extra work, her suggestions always led to an improvement in the product. Her willingness to allow me to bounce ideas and thoughts by her, made an incalculable difference.

I also need to thank a man I never met, Ethan Ellenberg. Ethan, who is a literary agent, took the time to read the first finished draft of this book. While his comments were favorable, he raised some issues, which changed the direction I was going. This led me to a complete rewrite of the manuscript. He was right - I had three books going on at once.

Another thanks goes to Steve Dworman, President of Informercial Marketing Report. Steve had discussed my book with Ethan and enticed him into reading it. If it had not been for Steve's introduction, I would not have had the benefit of Ethan's wisdom and suggestions.

A giant thanks goes to Richard G. Nixon, business man, publisher, fellow WINO and most of all, friend. He took time from his busy life to read the entire book and to make many good suggestions. Richard encouraged me in ways only a friend can. His ideas were backed by a lifetime of success and the knowledge he has gained.

A special thanks is due to my friend and colleague, Norma Barretta, Ph.D. Dr. Barretta took over the task of the final edit of this manuscript. She is uniquely qualified to do this. Norma not only taught English for many years, she is also an outstanding therapist.

To Skip Press, author of How To Write What You Want & Sell What You Write (Career Press-1995) and many other books, thank you for your guidance. Our lunches have been interesting and fun. Most of all, you have been free with your knowledge and time. You have been a great help.

# Disclaimer

This book is designed by the author and the publisher to provide information regarding the subject matter covered. It is sold with the understanding that the publisher and the author are not engaged in providing therapeutic, psychological, legal or other professional services. If expert assistance is required, you should seek competent professional services.

It is not the purpose of this book to present all the information that is otherwise available or could be available to the publisher and/or author. Instead, it is meant to complement, amplify and supplement other material available, in books, text and any other media generally available.

You are urged to seek other sources of information on the subject, including books, texts and the advice of others including competent professionals. This will allow you to tailor the available information to your specific needs.

Every effort has been made to make this book as accurate as possible. However, since it was written, edited and printed by humans, there **may be mistakes** in content and typographically. Therefore, the text should be used as a general guide only. It is not to be used as an ultimate source of information nor as the only approach that should or could be taken.

The purpose of this book is to entertain, educate and offer information for you to consider. H.I. Enterprises and the author shall have neither responsibility nor liability to any person, group or entity with respect to any loss or damage alleged to be caused, directly or indirectly, by the information contained in this book.

The proceeding disclaimer was required because of the legal climate (or perceived climate) that exists today. If you do not wish to be bound by the conditions written above, you may return this book to the publisher for a full refund.

INTRODUCTION

# *Relationship: Thy Name is often Misery*

'Tis the only comfort of the miserable to have partners in their woes' Miguel de Cervantes (1547-1616), Spanish writer. Don Quixote, pt. 1, bk. 3, ch. 10 (1605; tr. by P. Motteux).

When Cupid's arrow first strikes, we are most often too excited to notice just where the arrow has struck. We are too enraptured and carried away with the intensity of our feelings even to think about this little detail. It is only if the area of impact begins to become infected that we "sit up and take notice."

Too many couples find themselves in one crisis after another. Within these couples in crisis, at least one person is disappointed, unhappy, frustrated and often angry. Often, both are experiencing some or all these emotional states. Also, either or both may be acting abusively. This abuse is directed toward each other and toward themselves. It is often directed toward any children, unlucky enough to be around.

Most therapists now find themselves consistently involved with relationship problems. Often, many problems start out to be about one thing and turn out to be about the relationship. What therapists call a Presenting Problem, often turns out to be a symptom of a destructive relationship.

The above statements are not hyperbole. Just look around and you will see how true these statements are. Now add to your observations the following interesting fact: One of the fastest growing professions in the United States is that of Marriage - Family - Therapist. There has to be a reason.

We need to change how we view the subject of relationships. Contrary to the belief held by most people, a relationship has no life of its own. It has only the life people bring to it. When we begin to think of a relationship as simply the sum of all its parts, we will get closer to what a relationship is. Then, it becomes clear, that a relationship reflects all the parts each person brings to the relationship.

If the parts are well designed and fit together, the whole (relationship) will work. Most of the time, the relationship will run smoothly. Conversely, if the parts are in bad shape or if they are not made to fit together, then the whole (relationship) will not work very well. What is then created is a relationship filled with breakdowns.

The word relationship is simply the name or title given to situations where individuals come together for a common purpose. One synonym for relationship could be partnership. In business, a partnership describes the way the people have structured their relationship. The duties and obligations of the partners are different from what would be found within another structure, such as a corporation.

The word partnership, does not itself suggest if the partnership is one which will be successful or if it will fail. When we look at the word relationship in this way, we can understand how it (a relationship) can be neither good nor bad. It is a structure, which only describes the way people choose to be together.

Every relationship is like a mirror - it reflects the people who are in it. In an intimate relationship, we have two people sharing their lives together. If each person is basically happy, healthy and positive in outlook, there is a good chance the relationship will be happy, healthy and satisfying too.

If either or both of the individuals suffer from Destructive Relationship Syndrome, there is a good chance the relationship will be filled with many problems. Remember, a relationship is one form of partnership. If one or more of the partners fails to do his or her part, or cheats, lies, spends too much or (fill in the blanks with anything you can think of), the partnership will probably fail. A primary love relationship will also fail if either of the partners fails to carry out his or her responsibilities to the relationship.

This book may be one of the best gifts you have ever given to yourself. You will soon learn about ten specific factors, which can act as red (warning) flags for you. These ten factors suggest the presence of Destructive Relationship Syndrome. Besides these ten factors, I will mention other areas, which concern the course a relationship might take. Also, I will tell you about a few of the lies we have all heard.

As you find out more about the relationship lies we have been told, you may become confused. I will understand your confusion. After all, many of the lies I discuss are promoted by experts, in books, on Radio and Television. To give the devils their due, they really are experts. Too often, they are experts at failure and unhappiness. Why? Because these two areas are what most relationship experts study.

## Ten Factors to Consider

### 1. Domestic Violence

People who should care for each other are hurting each other instead! Police officials tell us that one of the most dangerous calls to answer is for a Domestic Disturbance. Studies show that domestic violence is on the increase.

### 2. Divorce Statistics

In some areas of the nation, fifty percent of *new marriages* end in divorce. These people thought they were in love and that love would be enough. Something has to be wrong.

### 3. Instant Relationships

Most of us spend more time deciding about which car to buy then in finding a mate. When we want to buy a car, we may get recommendations from friends and magazine articles, shop around and take test rides. Yet, many individuals will jump into a new relationship within days of meeting someone new. Sometimes, they jump within hours!

4. **Big Lie Number 1**

   Relationship experts tell us relationships are very hard work. Also, you must expect to be in a struggle to make a relationship work. They are wrong. The truth is, *destructive relationships make life hard.*

5. **Big Lie Number 2**

   This lie is directed toward those who are hoping to meet someone. You have been told that meeting people is hard to do. Books and courses tell you how, when and where to find someone you can meet. Meeting someone with whom you are compatible is not the problem. The challenge is in learning how to meet and recognize individuals who will be compatible and are in your best interest. Put simply, you must learn how to meet those people with whom a relationship has a good chance of working.

6. **Finding the "Wrong" Person**

   If you continue to find the *wrong* person, you may be suffering from Destructive Relationship Syndrome. As long as DRS controls your choices, you will continue to find the *wrong* person. This is one way that Destructive Relationship Syndrome prevents men and women from finding relationship success.

7. **DRS Warning Signs**

   There are clear warning signs, which alert you to the presence of Destructive Relationship Syndrome. When you learn these warning signs, you can avoid painful and destructive relationships. You will learn about these signs as you continue reading.

8. **"Instant Attraction"**

   What many people know as "instant attraction", may really be a warning of Destructive Relationship Syndrome. "Instant Attraction" relationships seldom work. They are nearly always filled with chaos and unhappiness.

9. **The Most Important Question**

   If you are not in a relationship, there is one question, more than any other, which you must ask and answer. Until you do this, you are not ready to be in a relationship. If you are in a relationship, this question can help you to make it a more successful one. This one question and its answer, can start you and your Significant Other on the road to a new and happier relationship life. You will find this question and its' answer in Chapter 10.

10. **The Most Common Mistake**

    Do you usually repeat the one common mistake, which often contributes to DRS? If you make this mistake, at a minimum, it will always affect your relationships in a negative way. Changing this one thing will lead to a more positive and healthy relationship. This common mistake is discussed in Chapter 2.

This book will take you on an interesting journey. Of course you will learn about the problems and traits, which make up Destructive Relationship Syndrome. What is more important, you will learn about many tools which will help you to create successful relationships.

Let us say you wanted to be a successful business person. Would you take an unemployed person, who has no assets, to lunch to learn about success? I doubt it. Yet, most people who have a history of unhappy relationships, do just that.

They get together with others who are just as miserable and unhappy as they are. Then, they compare notes and spend hours sharing their horror stories. Why not take someone to lunch who knows how to have a happy relationship? You will learn far more about what will work from this person.

I want this book to be a guide for you. I will take you step by step through Destructive Relationship Syndrome. Together, we will explore ways of being free from this condition. Also, I will offer many different methods and processes to aid you on your journey.

Your journey will take some time and effort. Let me assure you, the time and effort required is far less than what is required by a destructive relationship. As a bonus, you will give yourself an excellent chance of creating a happy, loving and successful relationship.

## Another Lie

Let me ask, "Is it true that practice makes perfect?" Most people would say, "Yes. Practice makes perfect." This is another lie the experts have told to us. The answer is no! What is true is that practice will increase the likelihood that what we practice, we will repeat as we have practiced it.

Think about what you have just read for a moment. If I practice hitting a tennis ball, repeatedly into a net, what will my results be? I will get really good at hitting the ball into the net. What I will not be good at is hitting the ball over the net nor will I be good at the game of tennis itself.

If for example, playing tennis is an important goal for me, I will need to take time to practice many small parts of the game. I would need to practice the serve, backhand, forehand, moving to the net and more. Also, I would need to put these pieces together into some coherent form. If I am patient and devote the necessary time in to it, I will soon begin to notice positive changes and improvement.

If you suffer from Destructive Relationship Syndrome, you have been practicing a painful game. You probably have become very adept at this painful game. Also, because of your practice, you have increased the probability you will repeat your patterns. If you have practiced these patterns for any length of time, they have probably become automatic and unconscious.

I am asking you to take time to learn what this book offers to you. You must take time to practice the new approaches, which this books suggests. If you will practice, you will soon notice some positive results. At a minimum, you give yourself a chance to reduce the stress and pain in your life and in your relationships.

When you break free of Destructive Relationship Syndrome, you will give yourself the opportunity to find or create a better relationship. A successful relationship is usually a happy relationship. Good relationships are satisfying and exciting in positive and constructive ways.

If you are in a relationship, what you learn may even be more important to you. What you learn can help you change an unsatisfactory relationship into one that works. You will also discover if your relationship is salvageable and worth putting in the time needed to make it better. Be warned: you may find out that your present relationship is not one you should spend more time and energy on. It may be too damaged to repair.

"One of the first business of a sensible man is to know when he is beaten, and to leave off fighting at once." (Samuel Butler, 1835-1902, English author. Samuel Butler's Notebooks, 1951).

### The Past:

*"If the only new thing we have to offer is an improved version of the past, then today can only be inferior to yesterday. Hypnotised by images of the past, we risk losing all capacity for creative change."*

**Robert Hewison** (b. 1943), British historian. *The Heritage Industry.* Intro. (1987).

CHAPTER 1

# *Destructive Relationship Syndrome: Myth or Fact?*

Are you frustrated and weary with relationships which just do not work? If your answer is yes, you are ready for this book. This book will introduce you to Destructive Relationship Syndrome or DRS. You are about to learn what Destructive Relationship Syndrome is. Also, you will learn what the causes and the danger signals of DRS are. You will also learn how to avoid DRS situations. I will give you many tools, which will show you how you can change your Destructive Relationship Syndrome patterns.

However, I want to warn you. This book is not an instant solution for all your relationship problems. Nor will it be a cure for all that ails you. While Instant Coffee, Tea and Oatmeal come very close to being instant, even they take some time and effort. For most of us, relationships are much more important than instant coffee. Therefore, you must be ready to dedicate time and effort if you want to break free of Destructive Relationship Syndrome.

No matter what text book you look at, you will not find Destructive Relationship Syndrome listed. Also, you will not find it listed in any psycho babble book, or in any diagnostic manual of psychological disorders. There is a good reason for its lack of appearance. *I recognized the condition and gave it a name.* That is why you will only find DRS defined in my book.

Please keep one idea in mind. I categorized the condition I have called Destructive Relationship Syndrome, based on over twenty-five years of working with couples, individuals and families. Add to this, nearly ten years of presenting seminars for those in the healing/helping professions. You see, I had a great deal of help in identifying this condition.

**Destructive Relationship Syndrome really exists.** Until now, no one has attached an official label to this condition. Yet, literally hundreds of thousands of individuals suffer, directly or indirectly, from this condition. Within a few pages, you will know if you suffer from DRS. By the time you have finished this book, you will also have the knowledge and the skills to break free of Destructive Relationship Syndrome.

I want to give you fair warning. It is not my intention to give you pablum. To put this into plain English, I will be blunt. This may cause some of you occasionally to take offense. This is fine with me. It is not my purpose to be your friend nor do I need you to think good things about me. My purpose is to give you an education in what is for most of us, a very important subject - *relationships*.

## Time, Effort and Money

Never in modern history, have so many put forth so much time, effort and money, in the pursuit of one thing – *A relationship that works*! Almost every week, a new seminar, program, or book is announced, which promises to solve all of your relationship problems. These promise to help you meet the right person, or to know just what to say and how to say it. Some programs promise to show you how to meet and marry a multi-billionaire. Others claim you will learn how to please your man or woman every time and in every way.

Yet, if you will take the time to talk to your friends, you will hear a recurring refrain. How hard they find it to meet the right person, or how unhappy their last relationship left them feeling. You may also hear how miserable their current relationship is making them.

As a topper, individuals who ought to know better, such as therapists, help perpetuate myths, which will lead you to more painful and unhappy relationships. You are being lied to, not only by the experts but often, by your friends as well. They may want to help but they are still leading you down the wrong paths.

While driving, I happened to hear a psychologist speaking on a local radio program. This reputed expert was discussing how relationships are always difficult. Also, she said that difficulty goes with the territory. She also said and I quote, "Every relationship is fraught with danger!" If we listen to her and people like her, what will we come to believe? We will need to conclude that being in a relationship is the same as being in a war!

The host of this radio show invited listeners to call in with their questions. Every caller was given the same message, albeit in different words. Relationships are painful and filled with stress. And what was this expert's advice? We must accept that every relationship is filled with upheaval. Since upheaval is typical of all love relationships, we must learn how to cope with constant upheaval.

I have a question for these experts. Why would a sane person want to be subjected to a life of upheaval and war? Make no mistake. Many experts talk about relationships and how to handle them as if they were in fact, a war. The goal of war is antithetical to a loving relationship. This does not stop most of the experts from promoting their ideas about war and relationships.

A few days later, I had the misfortune of hearing yet another expert expounding on relationships. He was offering his courses on "Know How to Fight and Win in Your Relationships"; "Using Anger to Make Your Sex Life More Exciting," "Winning the Relationship Wars," "Styles of Negotiations for the Modern Couple" and more.

I have altered the names of these programs, both to protect the guilty and to prevent a law suit. While the titles have been changed, the types of programs he was offering are illustrated by these titles. Today, more and more self-appointed experts are promoting these kinds of ideas. Why? I think it is because they believe all relationships are, by their very nature, chaotic and painful. Their advice is, *"Just get used to it and learn how to make war better."*

Thomas Hobbes (1588-1679) had this to say about war: "Force, and fraud, are in war the two cardinal virtues." (The Columbia Dictionary of Quotations,©1993 by Columbia University Press). As I am sure you can tell, I do not agree with what the experts usually have to say. I find it hard to believe that successful relationships can be built on a foundation, which is made up of "force" and "fraud."

## The Shrinks

There have been many studies, which have concluded that psychiatrists, psychologists and therapists in general, have poor interpersonal relationships. Even more, several studies have shown these groups are not doing too well generally. For example, members of these professions have high suicide rates and high rates of drug and alcohol abuse.

Lastly, people in these professions also manage to have very high divorce rates. Perhaps these factors play some part in the negative attitudes which are too often expressed about relationships by these experts. If these studies are close to being accurate, many of our experts are living painful, unhappy lives. This will no doubt distort their perceptions of what is possible or even normal.

If you wanted to learn how to play tennis or to fly, I know you would want to find a good instructor. Beyond the right credentials, you would also want someone who was successful at what he did. If it was tennis, you would want someone who can play the game and play it well.

You also will want him to be able to teach you the *tricks*, which will help you to become a good player. I find it hard to believe you would take lessons from someone who hated the game, played it poorly and was negative about the game to boot.

Yet every day, in every city in this country, individuals seek help from inept helpers. They often find therapists who cannot get along with their spouses or children and who evidence little or no joy in life itself. Often, they find themselves with people-helpers who believe life is unfair and whose lives and relationships are chaotic and unsatisfactory. It will not be easy to learn useful skills from those "experts" whose own lives are not working well.

We need another way. I hope what you read will cause you to begin to think in some new ways. Yet, this book is not meant to be the definitive answer, nor is it intended to solve all of life's problems. It is intended to give you a start in a new direction. A direction designed to help you leave chaos behind.

Instead of relationships which are chaotic and painful, I want to help you move toward finding and creating a happier and more satisfying relationship. Also, I want you to discover the methods of those individuals who already know the tricks, which help them to have good relationships. You will find out how you can be free from Destructive Relationship Syndrome. Once you are free of DRS, you will find yourself able to attract others who are also DRS free.

For those of you who are already in an ongoing relationship, the task may be different. You may or may not be able to use what you learn to make your current relationship into a good one. If the other person (your Significant Other or S.O.), is flexible and your relationship has not deteriorated into chaos, what you learn will definitely help. However, if your relationship is into severe chaos and it is almost ready to end, I am truly sorry. It is probably too late to for this situation to improve.

## Not Therapy

Before we travel much further, I want to emphasize one thing. This book is not to be considered therapy. It is not another, *"You can get it all together in only ten-minutes"* book. Instead, consider it a guide for the beginning of a new journey. Also, some of you may have more serious problems, which require professional help. For those, this book is still a substantial start toward moving in a healthier direction.

For most of you, the common sense in this book, along with the processes it contains, will give you many powerful tools.

With these tools, you can make a strong beginning on your new journey.

I have plans to introduce a seminar program based on this book and the couple seminars I have done. This seminar program will be a nuts and bolts program. It will not be a replacement for therapy. Instead, it will be an opportunity to interact with others who are on the road to better relationships. You will also be taught many specific processes, under supervision. While it will be work, it will also be fun. Believe it or not, it is OK to have fun while you learn.

If you wish information on seminars, or want to be on our mailing list to be notified about seminars see the last page of this book or contact the publisher H.I. Enterprises. We will send you our seminar schedule including the cities we will be visiting.

I would like to make an important point here. I do not want anyone to think good relationships are always free from strife. This is just not so. From time to time, couples have disagreements. However, this is a sometime occasion, not Standard Operating Procedure. Healthy couples handle these situations with grace and good will. They arrive at some workable solution and then get back to living life well.

Those couples who are in the throes of DRS do things in a way, which is unique to them. It is also the opposite of what successful couples do. These DRS couples can take a small disagreement and with skills known only to them, turn small problems into major wars. They then find just the right fuels to keep the fires of war going, until someone surrenders or both collapse from fatigue.

As an illustration, let us say you love to sail. As a competent sailor, you know your boat, the rules of the sea, how to read your charts and something about weather patterns. You recognize that occasionally you may run into an unexpected squall and that you must deal with it. However, most of the time, you find sailing a very rewarding experience.

If you knew that every time you went sailing you would hit a severe storm, would you really want to go on? How would you feel if you knew you would need to struggle to survive, almost every time you went sailing? Be honest with yourself. You would probably fall out of love with sailing. You might even consider giving it up. All the fighting and struggling would make sailing too painful for most of us. You might even come to hate sailing and everything related to it!

Too often, today's relationships are very much like sailing into a storm. They are chaotic, filled with arguments, put downs, power plays, manipulations and unpleasantness. To me, it is just like always sailing off into a storm and struggling to survive - and this is on a good day!

No wonder people are afraid and concerned. They look around at the couples they know and see pain. Often they see couples who seem to be serving a life sentence, in a cold, gray penitentiary. Often, people with failed relationships, cannot wait to tell everyone all the terrible details. When we hear these horror stories, is it any wonder we become afraid of being in an intimate relationship?

## The First Secret

Relationships need not be the way the experts or those with failed relationships describe them. I am going to make a statement, which many may disagree with. Those people who have learned how to have good relationships will agree but they may not be the ones reading this book. The first secret I want you to know is: *A Good Relationship is an Easier Way to Live*! Yes, I meant exactly what I said - *A Good Relationship Is an Easier Way to Live*. Later, I will illustrate my reasons for this statement.

The reason you may have difficulty with this concept is simple. You have been told too many lies about relationships. Like most of us, you have been brainwashed. I have already mentioned some of those lies. As I go along, I will mention more of the lies we have been told.

You now have the first secret for understanding Destructive Relationship Syndrome. This secret can help you to know if your current Significant Other or your relationship is a possible DRS situation or not. Ask yourself, "Is my relationship or my Significant Other making my life easier or more difficult?"

Your answer will quickly allow you to know what your current situation is. This question is a basic key to understanding the quality of any relationship or if your Significant Other is in your best interest. Simply put, if your relationship or your Significant Other is making your life more difficult, something is wrong. If you do not face the truth, it (the truth) will run you over. It is only a question of when.

## Cathy – Mr. Right?

Case histories are often a wonderful way for imparting information. I want to use one here, as a way of helping you to understand the importance of *Good Relationships Are an Easier Way to Live*! When you really grasp this idea, you probably can know, almost instantly, the quality of any relationship. This one bit of knowledge gives you an understanding, which most people do not have.

Cathy is a very bright, educated, attractive woman. She has a responsible position, and is believed to have a good future with the corporation she works for. Cathy is an avid skier, has many friends and is involved in social service activities. She is in her mid thirties and keeps in shape by regular workouts. Her life works and it works well, until she meets the ***right one***!

Cathy always knows when she has met the *right one*. She knows because the moment she meets him, she is strongly attracted to him. It does not matter that she knows nothing about him, his life or his values. He has a certain look and manner, which she finds irresistible. He is the candle and she is the moth. Cathy will do almost anything to meet him and she is, to her later regret, usually successful. (What happens to the moth when it is successful flying into the flame?)

On the first date or two, she is cautious. After all, her last two relationships ended painfully. Cathy tends to watch and listen to what is going on. She is committed to going slowly, while she observes. Also, she continues to see friends, engage in her usual activities and overall, lives her life well. Her life is working and is free from unnecessary complications. Slowly however, Cathy begins to slip into her patterns of Destructive Relationship Syndrome.

After several dates, Mr. Right made some sexist remarks about women. Cathy hates this kind of talk and thinks of herself as a liberated woman. Both of her last Mr. Rights were also given to making these kinds of sexist remarks. Her father often makes the same types of comments. She flat out hates this behavior. However, since she and Mr. Right have been getting along so nicely, she decides to let it slide. "After all, he was probably just joking."

Cathy now begins to let things slip in her life style. She forgets to call her friends and is even late with some of her work assignments. What the Hell. She and Mr. Right are spending more time together. To her, this is what is really important.

True, he is often late for their dates. Sometimes, he does not call her when he says he will. He might not even call her for several days. Cathy is quick to accept his explanations for these lapses. At the same time, she is spending more time wondering what her Mr. Right is up to. Her life is getting complicated and things are getting harder for her. She also begins to experience anxiety as her constant companion.

Cathy finds herself thinking about Mr. Right most of her waking hours. (Psychologists call this behavior obsessing). At this point, she begins to experience some swings in her mood. She feels very happy when she is with him, until he does something she does not like. Then she gets anxious and depressed. These feelings stay with her for longer periods.

When Mr. Right fails to call her, she finds herself worrying for hours and she is usually filled with dread about the future. She *knows* he has found someone else and is tired of her. In the real world, her work begins to deteriorate, bills go unpaid and she is miserable. Life grows more and more complicated and painful for her.

By now, Cathy has gone from being a competent, professional woman, to a poorly functioning wreck. She has difficulty sleeping and experiences periods of impaired concentration. Also, Mr. Right's treatment of her continues to become more cavalier and demeaning.

On a few occasions, he has called her names in front of other people. Her friends have made comments about this but Cathy is ready with a quick excuse for his behavior. "He has a lot on his mind"; "He doesn't mean anything by it" or "Well I did sound stupid."

While she will not admit it to anyone, Cathy wonders how she has found herself in an abusive relationship . . . again! She is totally convinced there is something really wrong with her. Also, she wonders why she always attracts this kind of guy. [She doesn't! Her DRS causes her to ignore men who would be in her best interest. Instead DRS leads her to respond to what fits her DRS best]. Her health is suffering, as is her work. For Cathy, life has become filled with stress and unhappiness.

Cathy is a real person. What you have just read is an accurate but edited account of her situation. This scenario has happened to her several times. It might be reasonable to ask, "Why does a successful, bright, attractive person, continue to get herself into such painful relationships?" This is what this book is about.

Destructive Relationship Syndrome often takes over a person's life. Then, like a Lemming, the individual marches right over an emotional cliff. Until the individual breaks out of DRS, he or she will find him or herself in one bad situation after another.

As you think about Cathy and what happened to her, remember our first secret: *A Good Relationship Is an Easier Way to Live.* We can see this rule lets us know her relationship was a bad one. The more deeply Cathy got into this relationship, the more difficult her life became. In short, this relationship caused her to lead a much more difficult life, in reality and emotionally.

Most of us are generally sane, at least in most areas of our lives. When it comes to relationships of the intimate kind, many individuals act as if they just caught a case of insanity. At best, they are without (common) sense. When they meet *that special person*, they go into a mental fog. What is more, they act as if their brain cells have fallen away and they end up "hooked."

None of this would be so bad, if a small majority of these relationships turned out to be successful.

The truth is this: today, too many intimate relationships do not work. Even where individuals choose to stay in a relationship, they often settle for being unhappy and dissatisfied. What is sad about this is that painful relationships can usually be avoided. Also, many ongoing relationships can be shaped into good ones – if only people knew how!

## Points To Remember

1. Much of what the experts tell us contributes to the pain and unhappiness of DRS.
2. This book is not therapy. It is a guide book to help you begin a new journey. I want this book to help you think about relationships in new ways.
3. A Good Relationship Is an Easier Way to Live! If your present relationship or Significant Other is causing your life to be more difficult, something is wrong.
4. If your relationship is causing you to let normal things slip and interfering with your friends and lifestyle, you need to step back. You need to take a good look at what is happening in your life. The sooner you do this, the sooner you will see what you need to do to make it better for you.

CHAPTER 2

# *Destructive Relationship Syndrome II Definition*

While it is not the purpose of this book to read like a psychology text, we do need a working definition of DRS. The following is my definition of Destructive Relationship Syndrome.

## Destructive Relationship Syndrome

A pattern, *generally recurring,* of seeking and/or finding individuals, with whom, in spite of initial attraction and appearance, you are truly not compatible, with whom your relationship is filled with problems, crises, arguments, chaos and poor communication. Such relationships often include verbal abuse and sometimes physical abuse.

Now I know the above is quite a mouthful. Relax. It is not necessary for you to memorize it. As we go along, I intend to take you through the definition one step at a time. I do not mean that every aspect must be present before an individual can be said to be suffering from DRS. Also, do not decide you suffer with DRS because you have had a bad relationship. It is the pattern of activities and behavior, which are important in determining the presence of Destructive Relationship Syndrome.

In Chapter 7, you will find an outline, which contains the key elements and patterns found in DRS. This outline will help you to have a solid grasp of the main aspects, which constitute Destructive Relationship Syndrome. You will also be given the opportunity to do one of two DRS self-evaluations. These evaluations will lead you to a better understanding of your own patterns.

I strongly recommend that you take the time needed to do this self-evaluation. The DRS outline and the self-evaluation, will each make much more sense after you finish this chapter. Please wait until you have finished this chapter before doing your self-evaluation.

## Robert and Betty – DRS Classic

You will now have the opportunity to study the case of Robert and Betty. This case study contains most of the elements found in DRS. When you have read this case, along with the DRS outline that follows, you will be well on your way to a basic understanding of DRS. By the way, I will often use case studies as a teaching tool. Not only do case studies make learning easier, they also make learning more interesting.

Robert and Betty were a classical example of a Destructive Relationship. Additionally, the history of each is a clear example of DRS. Both were gentle, nice and caring people in most areas of their lives. However, when it came to their important relationships with the opposite sex, things were not so hot.

Both had a history of getting into relationships, which were abusive. Both had gone through acrimonious divorces. As you read about Robert and Betty and how things unfolded, pay attention to how closely the case parallels the DRS definition you have learned.

Robert was a successful business man. He also invested in real estate with success. His professional history was exactly the opposite of his relationship history. In the business world, nearly everything he has tried has been successful.

When I met with him in my office, he owned two homes and a condominium near Waikiki, Hawaii. While not rich, he was well off and could retire, which he planned on doing within a few years. He was not quite ready to retire as he had a few business interests he still needed to liquidate.

With just one exception, each of his serious relationships with women ended in disaster. The one exception occurred when the lady and he recognized their relationship could not work. They decided to part as friends. Robert did admit he would have hung on to the situation, if the woman had not been so determined to end it. She was the only former Significant Other with whom he could maintain a cordial relationship.

Robert is a recovering alcoholic and nearly a Born Again Christian. When he and Betty met, Robert was very involved with his church and with many church activities. [He is still dedicated to his church and remains involved in church activities]. Betty knew of his church involvement but did not mention she seldom went to any type of religious activity.

When Robert turned forty, he decided he did not want to have children. This decision was made just before he met Betty. Robert was very good at keeping secrets and this was one of his secrets, which he kept very well. For some reason, he did not want Betty to know what his position about children was.

Betty is a vivacious type, who really loves socializing. Along with socializing, she likes to drink - a lot. Also, she is almost an atheist. She considered Robert's church activities as ".... kind of a waste of time." The truth was, she found religion a bore but kept this secret from Robert. As she put it, "I didn't mention these things because I didn't want to rock the boat. I really liked him."

Betty had a child from a previous marriage and had decided she wanted to have two more. When she met Robert, Betty was almost thirty-five years old. She was concerned her biological clock was running out and was very committed to the idea of having more children and quickly. Of course, she barely hinted at this because she did not want to cause a problem with Robert.

While Robert was about ready to retire from his active business activities, Betty was in the fast lane. She was determined to climb the corporate ladder and wanted to have a very active career. Betty looked forward to traveling for her company and wanted him to join her on these trips. Robert did not like business travel and did not want to be, as I said to him "a third wheel to a racing bike."

To add even more spice to the ingredients in this stew, Robert wanted to move away from California. Betty had most of her family, friends and business connections in California. As she said during one session, "I would never consider leaving my family." Betty was also very involved with her friends.

Before I forget, neither was fond of the other's friends. Each was sure things would be a lot better for the relationship, if only the other would just get rid of "his" or "her" friends. This had already become a source of consistent bickering.

By now, you might be wondering just how these two people got together? First, most of their differences did not come to the surface until after they began having sessions with me. Neither one had ever come close to asking the most important question all of us need to ask. [Never fear. I devote nearly a whole chapter to this question].

Both were careful to avoid most issues which might lead to any disagreement. They also tended to use typical DRS communication, which is not too helpful. Actually, they went out of their way to say only what they thought the other wanted to hear. To put it bluntly, they lied to each other about many things.

## Clear Differences

Betty had some good ideas about furthering her career. She had a basic plan regarding her career. In most other areas of life, she often let her emotions dictate her actions. This tendency affected her work performance and had a bad influence on her financial condition. As she was very spontaneous when it came to most things, she often went on binge buying sprees. When she and Robert met, Betty was deeply in debt because of her financial impulsiveness.

Robert wanted everything planned to the most minute detail. Doing anything new was an uncomfortable experience for him. He was also (what I might charitably call) frugal. Betty simply called him cheap. Of course, when it came to women, he was quick to jump out of an [emotional] airplane. He then would try to construct a parachute after he began falling.

Despite their differences, both had *very good reasons* for choosing each other. After all, she was tall, thin and blond, just like his first wife. As had been two other women with whom he had serious relationships. Robert and Betty both loved to ski and they liked the same kind of music. They had met at a party and he was instantly attracted to her. To quote Robert, "she looked just like my type."

She was impressed with the fact that Robert was a successful business man. He dressed well and he drove a BMW. This impressed her. Betty was also impressed that Robert owned his own business. His owning investment property impressed her too. She also liked his looks and how polite he was.

On their first date, they spent most of the night talking. What they mostly talked about was their former relationships and their former Significant Others. *This behavior is an important DRS red flag.* They discussed common childhood traumas and their parents too. I call this *game:* Mine Was More Painful Than Yours. This is another DRS Red Flag.

Many individuals who suffer from DRS act as if talking about problems, traumas and tragedies brings people closer to each other. They are wrong. Making these areas an important part of what they talk about is one of the most common mistakes a couple can make. At the minimum, this will have a negative impact on any relationship.

Anyway, this led them to discover they had a lot in common. His mother was a drunk and his home life had been full of unending battles. She, had a father who was a drunk and her parents were always at war with each other. To both of them, these similarities were good signs.

As you can imagine, it was not too long before they began to have problems in their relationship. In a very short time, they were often at war with each other about many things. During one of their big battles, a friend suggested they see me. Robert took the initiative and called to make an appointment with me. During this call, he said that both wanted the relationship to work.

## Foundation Issues

During our first session, I was able to bring into the open most of the substantial differences, which existed in their life styles and their goals. Also, both agreed they needed to lower the volume of acrimony in their relationship if anything positive was to be accomplished.

Both agreed they needed to find other ways of resolving the differences between them. However, I was candid in my assessment that their differences were, what I call, foundation or core issues.

Foundation issues either hold the whole structure (relationship) together, *or will cause it to collapse.* I also told them it would be hard work to change the types of foundation issues, which existed between them. I did not tell them I thought their prognosis was poor.

During our next meeting, their core differences became more apparent. As we discussed some new ways of communicating they began to hear each other, probably for the first time. By the end of this session, we had agreed on several issues which we needed to look at together. We also talked about how we would approach resolving them.

Two days later Robert called to cancel their next appointment. He was quick to point out that there was a very good reason for doing this. He told me that after discussing what they had learned in the session, they had decided they should elope! According to him, this would force them to work on the core issues. Both believed that being married would make the difference. I was less than pleased with their decision.

## The Honeymoon and The Disaster

After they eloped, they went on their honeymoon to Robert's condo in Hawaii. During the honeymoon, all Hell broke loose. Betty got drunk and physically attacked Robert. Their battle got so loud, someone called the police. The police were able to calm them down but this did not last for long. The next day Robert proceeded to fall off the wagon. He went on a drunken binge, which lasted for several days.

Several days later, Betty again got violent. This time Robert also got violent with her. He shoved her hard enough for her to bruise her head on a wall. She punched him several times. There was much screaming and lots of terrible things were said by both. This kept up until exhaustion finally caused them to stop.

After they sobered up, they decided it was time to get everything out in the open. Robert accused Betty of wanting him for financial reasons and because she wanted to get pregnant. Betty accused Robert of misleading her and only wanting her for a trophy wife. She expressed her disdain for his religious beliefs and his church involvement. Also, she told him she did not respect him because he was not ambitious enough.

Their anger began to spill over again. Robert turned his back on Betty and walked out while she was still talking. He disappeared for several days. While he was gone, Betty got even more upset with Robert and the situation too. Without leaving any word, she left Hawaii and went home to her family. I could go on but I have a low tolerance for pain.

Anyway, they stayed together on and off, more or less, for a little over one year. During this time, they sought help from his church and two marriage counselors. [Robert told me later that they were too embarrassed to come back and work with me.] While in therapy, they became even more verbally abusive with each other. There were more incidents, which led to verbal abuse by both of them. Several incidents came close to physical violence.

This unhappy situation was ended by a messy divorce. [Keep in mind that all divorces are messy. Some are just more messy then others]. The lawyers did well and Robert and Betty survived, sort of. If you do not count all the emotional pain, lost time, bitterness and the costs, financially and otherwise, they did OK.

Welcome to the wonderful world of Destructive Relationship Syndrome! This case contains a plethora of DRS patterns. While the case of Robert and Betty may seem extreme, it is not so unusual. While it may not match your situation, you can learn from it. It is a very educational example, because it contains so many factors found in DRS.

As an aside, Robert decided to break his pattern of Destructive Relationship Syndrome. He began having sessions with me on a regular schedule. I asked him to agree to stay out of relationships until he was well on the road to mastering the skills needed for a healthy relationship. Robert did sell his business interest and continued his work with me.

He also continued to be active in his church and its many activities. After nearly a year, he met a woman who shared many of his core values. At the time I wrote this, he had been in a *sane* relationship for about eight months.

Betty found another Mr. Right before her divorce from Robert was final. Two weeks after meeting the new Mr. Right, they moved in together. She blamed Robert for the whole messy situation and refused to admit her contributions or her problems. Shortly after the divorce was final, she and Mr. Right were married.

Mr. Right had recently been busted for Driving Under the Influence (DUI). One night, he got so angry that he threw a telephone at her. Betty did not let these things dissuade her one bit. All in all, a sad ending for her. It was also the start of a new Destructive Relationship Syndrome drama.

As I was writing this chapter, I happened to hear a commercial on a local radio station. The announcer, while discussing the product he was selling, said that people have married after knowing each other less than two weeks. He went on to say that therefore, two weeks should be plenty of time to discover if the product he was selling, was as wonderful as the maker says it is.

He then said, "If not, return the . . . for a full refund. No questions asked and no hassles." Well good people, you do not get out of relationships so easily! There is always a great number of costs and hassles. Most important of all, two weeks may be long enough for a person to decide if the advertised product is what he wants. Please believe me when I say, it takes longer than two weeks to learn about another person.

## What about Love at First Sight?

Yes. What about Love at First Sight or as someone else called it, Lust with Possibilities? I have every intention of addressing this important and exciting subject. Before I get to it, we need to discuss a few other topics. Be patient and your questions about Love at First Sight will be answered. At the very least, you will have some new questions about this subject.

## Points To Remember

1. The DRS definition: The short version - A pattern of painful and unhappy relationships.
2. It is important to the success of a relationship that you are honest with your Significant Other - particularly about those areas where there could be disagreement between you.
3. Ending a relationship is always painful and often expensive too. Only the Lawyers do well. OK, so do therapists.
4. Pay careful attention to the differences, which exist between you. If they are foundation or core issues, be careful. Ask yourself, "Can these core differences *realistically* be resolved?"
5. Be sure to ask yourself, "Are your styles of leading life compatible, complementary or in conflict?"
6. Slow Down! It takes time to learn about and know about someone. Until you really know a person, you cannot possibly make an intelligent decision about what kind of person he or she is.

CHAPTER 3

# *In the Beginning*

Earlier, I promised you that this book would not be a book filled with *psycho babble*. Also, that it would not be dedicated to therapy issues. I intend to keep these promises – almost. I believe that some understanding about the origins and general causes of Destructive Relationship Syndrome will be educational. Education is what this book is all about. If, besides being educational, this information helps anyone to break free from Destructive Relationship Syndrome, then I am pleased that I have partially broken my promises.

## A Little Parable

Once upon a time, not so long ago, there lived a young man who, deep inside, did not like himself very much. Along his journey through life he had picked up several unpleasant ideas about who he was. He was afraid he was not smart enough, successful enough or worthy enough to deserve being loved by anyone. Also, he lived in fear of being *found out*, whatever this meant to him. He tried to hide who he believed he was from everyone.

Meanwhile, there lived a young woman, who in spite of being attractive, witty and bright, also feared she would be unmasked. She was sure once people got to know her, they would discover she was not someone anyone could ever really love. This belief led her to live in fear that people would discover "the truth" about her. She did everything she could to avoid places, situations and people, which might lead to her being exposed as an unlovable fraud.

The young man and woman dreamed of finding someone whom they could each love and who would love them in return. Yet when it came time to search for someone, they would find excuses such as, "It's too hard to find anyone in this city," or "All the really good ones are taken," or "I'm so busy, I just do not have the time to find someone." Truths be told, each was afraid of being rejected.

No one looks forward to being rejected, at least no one who is sane. However, when you like yourself, you know you can survive rejection. You know you will be OK if it should happen. Also, you are confident that you will find someone with whom you will really connect. When you do not like yourself, rejection takes on a very different face. If you do not like yourself, rejection feels almost like getting run over by a tank and you are afraid it is forever.

When it came time for the young man to search for a mate, his fear of rejection took over. This led him to avoid those women who were confident, successful and happy. They really frightened him and he *knew* they would not want someone like him. Of course, he never admitted this to anyone, especially to himself. Instead, he convinced himself these women were unattractive and not the kind of women he wanted.

With his self-delusion in full control, he found himself drawn to women who were at the very least as insecure as he was. It was even better if they were more insecure, if such a state was possible. He reasoned that if a woman **needed** him, she would overlook all of his faults. His search for a mate began to narrow down to finding someone who was needy enough, to accept him in spite of all his perceived faults.

Meanwhile the young woman had developed a unique skill. She was able to *not see* any man who was not at least as unhappy as she was. This skill allowed her to spot almost instantly, any number of men who suffered from any combination of DRS in Disguise [See Chapter 4]. If these men were also poor at communication and seldom said what they really meant, they were even more interesting to her.

Then one day it happened - they met. And it was Love at First Sight (See Chapter 6). Very quickly, they were married. Soon their troubles began and then escalated. As their marriage became noisier, more unhappy and filled with tension, they decided to have a baby. They reasoned (if we can call what they did reasoning) that a baby would bring them back together.

## Enter the Baby

When the baby was born, they were happy - for a short time. Initially, they made efforts to be good parents. Since the baby was helpless, they went out of their way to be loving and to take good care of the baby. Because the baby was so dependant on them, they felt secure. The baby could not leave them. This allowed them to be open, loving and caring parents.

Then things began to change. The baby was no longer a baby but began to walk and talk and to say "NO!" To parents as insecure as these, the baby's "no" was more than simply a no. To them, hearing the baby's "no" was a warning of what they feared was yet to come.

What do insecure people fear more than anything? *Rejection.* To these parents, the baby's "no" was the start of the baby turning on them. In their minds, this meant that one day, he would surely reject them. It was only a matter of time.

## Four Painful Strategies

There are certain strategies insecure people use when they feel threatened. One of the most common is, *I will reject you before you can reject me*! If the parents in this parable choose this course, they will become cold, distant and usually, too busy to be with the child. They will usually act as if the child is unimportant and often a nuisance.

This strategy causes a child to conclude, "I am not lovable. Even my own parents do not want me. If my own parents do not love me, then I know no one else will ever love me either. I will be all alone and no one will want me."

Another strategy insecure people use, could be called, *Suffocate them with love.* With this method, the parents do everything for the child. They never let the child learn to do or think for himself. Under the guise of being so *loving,* they do everything for the child. This reduces the child to being a pseudo helpless person. The message to the child is simple. *Without us, you cannot do anything. You will never make it in the real world. You will always need us because you are helpless. Now, you can never leave [reject] us.*

The message also means: You are helpless and a victim of the world. You cannot survive without us (or someone) to take care of you and protect you. We will protect you by doing everything for you. If you ever leave us, you will be all alone and unloved. No one would be there to help and protect you. You are lucky we are here to do these things for you.

To this, a child might add, "I better not say or do anything, which would cause my parents (protectors) to be angry with me. If they get angry with me, they may not protect me. I must do what they want and make sure I always please them."

Another choice might be to continually test the parents. By testing, I mean getting into trouble, at home, at school and everywhere else. With this choice, the child becomes "The Problem Child." Why would the child choose this course of action? One reason might be to see if the parents can really be counted on to offer the protection they have implied would be there.

A third strategy used by insecure parents calls for them to become overly critical of nearly everything the child might attempt. No matter how well the child does, they always find something wrong with it. With this strategy, the implicit message is this: *You are so inept that you cannot possibly make it on your own. Since you need us to show you the right way, you can never leave [reject] us. If you leave us, you may not be able to survive.*

With the third method, a child concludes he is really a bad (inept, stupid, impotent) person. As such, he is lucky to have anyone. He will believe he must hang on at all costs. This can lead him to bury his individuality and attempt to be whatever anyone wants him to be. Too often, the third method leads to self hate.

Self-hate can lead to self-destructive actions: drug addiction, prostitution, criminal activity, violence and a host of other problem behaviors.

The fourth possibility is even more damaging than what you have already read. Here, the parents of the child in our little parable combine bits and pieces of all three methods. The mother may take one part, say *Smothering With Love,* while dad takes, *I will reject you before you can reject me.* Dad may choose *Smothering With Love* while mom chooses *You cannot do anything right!* The combinations are myriad!

Whichever combination of strategies the insecure parents choose, you can well imagine the effects on the child. Will a child grow up feeling good about himself or filled with self-doubt and self-hate? It is likely the latter will be the case. "After all, parents are always right," the child concludes.

Once the damage is done, what kind of mate will he seek? It has been said that self-esteem, like water seeks its own level. This is why patterns can repeat themselves again and again. Each succeeding generation learns how to be better at Destructive Relationship Syndrome. Because of this, it is probable he will seek out a mate whose self-esteem (self-hate) matches his own.

Most, if not all individuals who suffer from DRS, developed their patterns while growing up. It is not my intention to cast stones at parents or any primary caretaker. However, to better understand the patterns of Destructive Relationship Syndrome we must examine the types of environments which may lead a child to develop Destructive Relationship Syndrome.

What I have described in The Little Parable gives us a start toward this understanding. I want to describe some additional situations, which will help you have a better understanding of how DRS can come about. Any one or any combination of the situations you have read and will read about, plays an important role in how well or how poorly we do with our relationships.

## The Addictive Family

So much has been written about addiction and *Dysfunctional Families* that I run the risk of being one more little noise in an already very loud debate. No matter how much I add to the din, we must recognize that alcohol, drug abuse and the chaos, which results from these, all contribute mightily to the development of Destructive Relationship Syndrome.

An individual raised in an environment poisoned by drugs and booze, will find it difficult to learn any healthy relationship patterns. This is simply common sense.

The types of communication found within addictive families are often confusing and crazy making. A child may grow up having learned to communicate only with others who have been raised in the same type of environment. Put this together with what you learned from The Little Parable. You can clearly predict what the results will be.

Additionally, in the Addictive Family, denial and avoidance of reality are the foundations by which the family functions. In this environment, seeing the contradictions and questioning them generally results in pain to the person who raises the questions. To survive in this environment, the child also learns to engage in denial and avoidance. Soon, he becomes good at denial and avoidance.

He carries his ability for denial and avoidance into his adulthood. These become part of the way he deals with life. He may not even give his denial and avoidance a second thought. As a result of this there is an inability to see what is really happening and a strong tendency to seek out someone who came from the same world.

## Violence

Violence often goes hand in hand with an Addictive Family environment. Of course there can be violent families without addiction. Also, there can exist Addictive Families without the presence of violence. Usually however, the two are found together. Even a cursory look at the news, shows how often violence is linked to some kind of substance abuse.

When there is violence in the family, a child is often told that the violence is OK. This message may be given by words or by the actions and attitudes of the people who are violent. Even worse, the child may be told the victim is responsible for this violence. It is not uncommon for an abused person to agree with this position.

Sometimes children are told, usually by an abused mother, "When daddy hits me, he's just showing how much he loves me. Besides, I shouldn't have upset him." Hearing this, a male may grow up with a belief that using force on members of your family is acceptable. He may believe it is also an expression of love. "Mom and Dad accepted it, so it must be OK."

A woman raised in a violent home may unconsciously seek out men who will show *love* by hitting them. I have had several women say to me, "I know he shouldn't hit me but at least I know he cares." One woman told me she did not like to date nice men. She said, "When I date nice guys who don't lose their tempers and hit me, how can I know if they really care about me?"

These abusive men are not showing love. They are exercising control, expressing inappropriate anger or acting out their fears about women. I am not saying abusive men do not feel love. What I am saying is that these men are filled with rage and fear. This rage and fear are what controls them. These feelings overwhelm whatever love, caring and compassion they are capable of still feeling.

Often, individuals raised in an Addictive Family Environment find normal, healthy relationships to be boring. This is particularly true if their family life also included violence. As one man said, "I know our relationship is crazy and we often hit each other, but at least it's always exciting!" So too, is playing Russian Roulette with a bullet loaded in every chamber but one.

## Unfinished Business

As we have seen from A Little Parable, being raised in a chaotic environment will lead a person toward becoming filled with self-doubt and often self-hate. This often leads to a deep gut wrenching fear that one cannot be loved. This is a painful way to go through life. Most people will try to do something about it. Often, they end up repeating the very conditions which caused them such pain in the first place. I think this is because we seem to have a drive toward attempting to complete the unfinished business from our past.

Imagine a young girl who concludes, accurate or not, she was not loved by a parent. As I said above, this may persuade her to decide, "if my own mother (or father) can't love me, then no one will ever love me." Once she makes this decision, she often will attempt to change the situation by getting the parent(s) to love her. Her underlying belief might be: "If I can get my mother/father to love me, I can believe that someday, someone else will love me."

No one wants to believe they can never be loved. It is simply too painful to accept. This is why the girl sets out to get the parent(s) to become loving. This is something like trying to get a piano to dance. It is highly improbable. Almost all of her energy and efforts go toward *proving* to the parent(s), she is worth loving. Of course, nothing changes.

If the parent(s) knew how to be more loving, the parent(s) would have acted differently in the first place. The parent's own insecurity prevents this outcome. Anyhow, the young girl keeps on trying to get what she can probably never get from that parent: some evidence of being loved by that parent. Instead, she gets more of what she has always received from that parent. Each failure to get some evidence of being loved only drives home more deeply her sense of being unlovable.

As time goes on, the girl becomes a young woman. She may now unconsciously seek out someone just like the rejecting parent(s). Her goal is still the same: *To win the love of the parents*. Only now, she attempts to achieve it through a substitute. Since the person chosen is very much like the rejecting parent(s), we can predict the results - more rejection. The harder she tries to complete the unfinished business of her past, the more likely she will be to produce a replay of that past.

For a few individuals raised in such an unloving environment, the results are even more devastating. They may have an absolute acceptance they can never be loved. As a result, they may simply give up. These individuals can become reclusive, or severely damaged psychologically. They will often experience depression.

Occasionally, a few of these people may even become sociopaths. They may become violent toward society. Their way of finishing unfinished business is to get even! We may read about these people, when they attack and hurt and too often, kill innocent people.

## Self-Fulfilling Prophecy

This is another subject discussed and written about extensively. How it relates to the subject of relationships has not been widely discussed. Yet, Self-Fulfilling Prophecy can have a strong impact on the kinds of people we are drawn to and the kinds of relationships we find ourselves in.

Let's say a young boy named Sam, is being raised by a bitter, unhappy and frustrated parent. Imagine the parent takes out frustration on Sam by calling him stupid almost every day. Sometimes, not only is Sam called stupid, he is also hit because of the behavior the parent considers to be stupid.

While Sam is a young boy, he has no way of knowing his parent is the one with the problems. Instead, Sam, like all young children, assumes his parent must know everything. Therefore, Sam must truly be stupid or his parent would not say so.

Sam hears it so often, it becomes a big part of how he sees himself. He comes to believe he is indeed, stupid. Based on what he believes about himself, he begins to predict how his life will be. What he sees in his future does not look pleasant.

Since Sam now *knows* he is stupid he also figures out it will not do any good to pay attention in school. After all, stupid people cannot learn. Sam daydreams in class, avoids homework and often gives dumb answers when called on in class. To Sam, his dumb answers and the snickers of his classmates, is more proof of his stupidity. Of course the dumb answers are a result of Sam not listening or even really being present in the class, except in body. It has nothing to do with his intelligence but he does not know this.

Sam's grades reflect his lack of attention and effort. Of course his grades *prove* to him he is stupid. He drops out even more and learns even less while continuing to prove the prophecy. Now add the following questions: What kinds of kids does Sam seek out as his friends? How will Sam look upon the world in general? What will Sam believe he deserves from life or in a career?

Soon, Sam's world will be made up of painful experiences. His friends will see the world as he does. He will become an expert at avoidance of all situations and people, which will make his stupidity all the more evident, at least in his eyes. By the time Sam is in high school, he has completely dropped out, either in spirit or in reality.

When Sam attempts to get a job, he finds because he is a dropout, there are very few jobs available to him. He finds himself with a low paying, low skilled job. This only adds to his lousy self-image. It reinforces his belief that all this is happening because he is stupid. In his mind, if he were not stupid, he would not have to settle for a crummy job.

Every time Sam thinks about improving himself or takes steps to do so, he is filled with anxiety. If he attempts to follow through, such as returning to finish school, his anxiety overwhelms him. He either avoids starting school, or drops out after he starts. Either way, he is continuing to live up (or is it down) to his poor self-image. Each day, Sam continues to live out his Self-Fulfilling Prophecy.

As you read about Sam, you can see how his Self-Fulfilling Prophecy could control his life. Let me add to this metaphor the following question: What kind of relationships can Sam look forward to? I am sure he will avoid women whom he sees as smarter than he is. With his belief system, this will include nearly all women. He will probably find himself with someone whose self-esteem is just as low if not lower than his. More of his Self-Fulfilling Prophecies coming true.

Where an individual is told repeatedly, "You're just like your . . .," or "Life is a struggle and nothing will ever come easy," or "You'll never amount to anything," or "What's the matter with you? Can't you do anything right?" and dozens more, the die is cast. A person who comes to believe these things, will often grow up and recreate what he or she has learned to believe.

Without doubt, Self-Fulfilling Prophecy plays an important role in the formation of Destructive Relationship Syndrome. When you link Self-defeating beliefs with Self-fulfilling Prophecy, watch out! This is a potent combination for disaster.

If for example, we come to believe we are just like a certain parent, we may grow up emulating this parent. We will also probably seek out a mate who is similar to the one this parent had. If our parents were chaotic and their relationship was bad, guess what? We can end up recreating just what we grew up with. Of course if our parents were healthy and had a good, productive, happy relationship, this would produce a good result.

When we add Self-Fulfilling Prophecy to finishing Unfinished Business, we have created a breeding ground for DRS. Between lousy self-esteem, which goes with a negative Self-Fulfilling Prophecy and the tendency to recreate our past with the hope we can get it to come out differently this time, we can create total havoc for our lives. In effect, where an individual is driven by these factors, he is like an automaton. He is almost compelled to carry out his old, painful programming.

[For more on how beliefs control us see "Monsters and Magical Sticks: There's No Such Thing as Hypnosis", Heller and Steel, New Falcon Publications, 1987]

## Ending the Beginning

If you were unfortunate enough to come out of a chaotic, unhealthy and unhappy environment, you need to be on your guard. The patterns I describe throughout this book are often unconscious patterns. As such, they may be hard to recognize or change.

By becoming conscious of any patterns you may have, you will put yourself in position to make important, powerful, healthy changes in your life.

When you finish this chapter, I recommend you set aside thirty minutes to an hour. During this time, review what kind of environment you were reared in. Look for a history of any of the following:

1. Harsh, Judgmental and Rigid Parenting
2. Mixed and often *Crazy* Communication
3. Cold, Rejecting Parent/s
4. Booze and/or Drug Abuse
5. Being Treated as if Unimportant, Being Discounted
6. Violence, with or without Substance Abuse
7. Sexual Abuse
8. Suffocating Love
9. Traumatic Divorce
10. Consistent Yelling and Arguing [Verbal Violence]

Along with any of the above patterns, also make an effort to identify negative Self-Fulfilling Prophecies, which are active in your life now. Please keep in mind what a potent combination Self-Fulfilling Prophecy and Unfinished Business can be. You may be shocked to find out how much you are controlled by these two things.

Until we break free of Unfinished Business and our negative Self-Fulfilling Prophecies, our lives will be filled with pain and disappointment. Also, we will often help create unhappy relationships. In many ways, trying to finish Unfinished Business while acting on our negative Self-Fulfilling Prophecies throws more fuel on an already raging fire.

In Chapter 12, I will offer you three methods that are specifically designed to change your negative beliefs. I call one method, Three for One. This technique can help you become more positive in your communication toward others and internally too. Three for One can help you make a positive change in how you think about yourself as well

I call the other methods the Blackboard Technique and Flash Cards. These methods can help you to change your deep-seated negative beliefs. Also, Flash Cards help you learn to respond in new ways to everyday situations. Often, these two methods help a person to change his Self-Fulfilling Prophecies. Used together, these three methods can lead to important changes for you.

## Points To Remember

1. The Four Parenting Strategies, which contribute to Destructive Relationship Syndrome: I will reject you before you can reject me; Suffocate with Love; The Critical Parent; A combination of all three.
2. If you were raised within an Addictive or Violent Family you are at risk of recreating the same situation in your present relationships.
3. When we combine Unfinished Business, with a negative Self-Fulfilling Prophecy, we usually create unhappy relationships.
4. Many of the patterns, which negatively influence our relationships, are unconscious. It is in your best interest to make them conscious. This makes it easier to change them.
5. One step toward Ending the Beginning is to look at the kind of family environment in which you were reared. Look for any history of the ten situations you read about earlier in this chapter.

CHAPTER 4

# *DRS in Disguise*

Destructive Relationship Syndrome comes in many shapes, styles and forms. Usually, it is not nearly as obvious as you might expect. Often, DRS is even hidden behind attitudes and behavior which can seem normal or even laudable. It is the conscious or unconscious motives of the actor that often determines whether the behavior is that of someone with healthy behavior or someone who is trapped in Destructive Relationship Syndrome.

> "We should often be ashamed of our finest actions if the world understood all the motives behind them." (François, Duc de La Rochefoucauld (1613-80), French writer, moralist. Sentences et Maximes Morales, no. 409 (1678). The Columbia Dictionary of Quotations, Columbia Press.

I know it is very difficult to unearth the secret intentions of another person. It is often not possible to know what his motives are. There is another factor, which can complicate the whole subject of intentions. Often, the actor himself is unaware of what his real intentions are. This is an example of what denial often can create.

I have told you how dangerous denial can be. DRS in Disguise is an area where denial can be devastating. If you are in denial or attempting to avoid dealing with your personal issues, it will be hard for you to uncover your own motivations. Until you know what motivates your actions, it will be hard to change them.

As you read about the many disguises of DRS, I know it will become easier for you to recognize many familiar patterns. You may come upon patterns which you have engaged in. Some patterns may remind you of someone else. I want you to keep in mind, *"The Truth Shall Set You Free!"* First, it may get you angry.

## The Crutch and the Crutchie

Have you ever known anyone who has broken her leg and had to rely on a Crutch as a result? If you have, you also know how quickly she developed a conflict toward her Crutch. On one hand, she was dependant on it and was probably afraid to go anywhere without it. Conversely, she developed a strong disliking for the Crutch. She probably could not wait to get rid of it.

When she could, she would put the Crutch somewhere it would be inconspicuous. This might be in a corner or even in the trunk of her car. As she gained more confidence in her ability to get by without the Crutch, she moved it into the garage. After a little while, she gave it away. Goodby Crutch!

I want you to imagine how a Crutch might think and feel about all of this, assuming a Crutch could think and feel. First, the Crutch has to spend its useful life with an armpit draped over it. Next, the Crutch knows if it does a good job, its reward will be separation followed by total abandonment.

If however, the Crutch fails to do its job, its fate will still be the same. Also, whether it does a good job or if it fails, the crutch will be hated. I do not know about you but were I a crutch, I would surely find this kind of life to be stressful at best and awful at worst.

When it comes to the Crutch and Crutchie, you will find two parties combining to create what I have just described. One person sees himself as crippled, while the other believes she must hold the first one up. The conflicts, which I described earlier, will soon rear their many heads.

The Crutchie is someone who has learned to believe, consciously or unconsciously, there is only one way to get someone to care for him. It is to be weak and dependant. The Crutchie seeks out and finds someone who will play the Crutch. However, almost from the beginning, the Crutchie begins to feel resentment toward the Crutch for the *control* the Crutch appears to have over him. This resentment soon turns into anger and hostility.

Most therapists believe that anger, unexpressed and turned inward, often leads to depression. As I put it, depressed people often direct their anger against the only person they believe is too weak to fight back. Anyway, it is common for the Crutchie to slip into depression. Other possibilities include the Crutchie *acting out* his anger through rage, withdrawal, sexual withholding, stubbornness, sabotage, etc.

At this point, the Crutchie begins to suspect that the Crutch is the wrong person for the job. After all, "If she really cared, I wouldn't feel so bad." Also, the Crutchie begins to experience anxiety because the protection hoped for is not working. The Crutchie begins to believe he is now vulnerable and unprotected. Soon, he begins shopping for a new and better Crutch.

Now, let us examine the life of the Crutch. She believes love will be given to her, only if she allows someone to lean on her. In her mind, her role is to hold up a Crutchie and make him safe. She must also have all the right answers to boot. This would be a big job for Super-woman. It is way too big a job for a mere mortal. In spite of these problems, the Crutch is *drawn* to Crutchies, like flies to flypaper.

Within a short time, the Crutch begins to feel the stress and strain of carrying another person. As the Crutchie begins to express anger or gets worse by getting depressed, The Crutch begins to get bitter. "All this work and all I get are more problems. I never get any love or gratitude," are typical thoughts of the Crutch.

On the other hand, if the Crutch manages to help the Crutchie get stronger, another set of problems will arise. The Crutchie will begin to build a new life. This could include such things as going back to school or getting a better job. Also, the Crutchie will find new friends and associates and spend time with them. The Crutch begins to feel abandoned and is afraid the Crutchie will soon find someone else to be with.

Quickly, the Crutch begins to experience more resentment and anger. "Look at all I have done for you and this is how you repay me! How can you treat me this way?" Now, you have two angry, frustrated and miserable people. Each blames the other for violating their unspoken agreement. The relationship will become more chaotic and will probably end and end badly.

Since the Crutch/Crutchie is a Destructive Relationship Syndrome pattern, each will go out and repeat their part of the equation. The results will always be the same but this will not stop either. Each will believe the next Crutch or Crutchie will be the right one.

## The Savior and the Lost Soul

This pattern is similar to the Crutch and the Crutchie. The main difference is the degree of the behavior involved. In this pattern, one individual has cast herself in the role of a Lost Soul. Her life will be filled with disaster and unhappiness. She is generally without money or a job. Often, she is already in some very painful situation - an abusive relationship for example.

Sometimes she is a practicing drunk, drug addict or has some other addictive behavior. While she is playing the Lost Soul, she will not be in a recovery program, at least not actively. She may have a recurring problem with depression, anxiety attacks or eating disorders. Her life history will be replete with unhappy events, including her relationships.

The Savior is just that. This individual seems to have a compass which automatically locks onto all Lost Souls. Once a Savior finds a Lost Soul, the Savior jumps in to save the Lost Soul. When the Lost Soul is a drug addict, the Savior attempts to *get her off the stuff.* Where the Lost Soul is in a bad relationship, which is nearly always, the Savior will attempt to get her out of the relationship.

If the Lost Soul is suffering from psychological problems, the Savior may become her *shrink*. Where the Savior gets the Lost Soul into therapy, the Savior will often attempt to direct the therapy from the sidelines. This is because saving is the Savior's job.

If the Lost Soul is depressed, the two of them will spend literally all their spare time talking about the Lost Soul's problems and depression. Nearly all other aspects of their lives will come to a stop. The Savior and the Lost Soul patterns are almost full time jobs for both.

What I have been describing are the high points of this pattern. It gets worse! The Lost Soul usually believes pity equates with love. She may have only seen or experienced caring during crises or when someone was in pain. This led her to develop a personal metaphor that says "to be loved I must be unhappy and my life must be a mess!" The Lost Soul is expert at creating this.

The Savior has learned to equate love with acting like a Savior. This individual very seldom would experience *normal* love, caring or affection. Instead, somewhere in his history, he was taught the way to show love is to take care of someone who has problems and is really miserable. Usually, the Savior saw very little love or affection except for someone saving someone else.

## Becoming a Savior

I worked with a woman whose father had been severely depressed for years. He had tried to commit suicide several times. When he got depressed, her mother would drop everything to save him. It was only during these times of *saving* that her parents appeared close. Her mother often told her, "This is what a woman does, if she loves her man."

The daughter was a very good student. When she grew up, she could easily find depressed, unhappy men. When she found one, she would drop everything to jump in and save him. This is what a woman does to show love was the lesson she had learned. If it was good enough for her mother, it is good enough for her.

She would find a man who was out of work and heavily in debt. Then, she would lend him money and help pay off his debts. If a guy was a drinker, she would cover up for him. This included lying for him and to herself. And the beat went on and on.

Where a couple is operating with this Destructive Relationship Syndrome pattern, they will be in turmoil nearly all of the time. The Lost Soul must continue to be lost so she can be loved according to this metaphor. Meanwhile, the Savior's metaphor says one is only loved for saving someone. The result of this pattern is a relationship in a crisis, coming out of one, or getting ready for the next crisis.

As if what I have said were not sad enough, there is more. This pattern generally prevents either person from having a very successful career or personal life. There just is not enough time or energy left over for either. This lack of time and energy separates this pattern from the Crutch/Crutchie pattern. Lost Souls are almost nonfunctional and their lives are nearly a total disaster. The Crutchie on the other hand, is generally able to function fairly effectively but needs to be propped up to do so.

## The Therapist and the Patient

Here again, there are many similarities to the patterns I have previously described. One distinguishing characteristic makes this a separate pattern. It is the *clinical* nature of the relationship. One person is designated the Patient and has psychological problems or unresolved personal issues. The other person takes the role of the Therapist. The Therapist attempts to analyze and produce a cure for the *Patient's* problems.

Even if the Patient is in therapy, the Therapist will continue to do *"extra-curricular therapy"* with the Patient. Often, the Therapist will interfere with actual therapy. If the Patient is not in therapy and should seek out professional help, it will cause problems for the couple. The *Therapist* feels threatened by this development. He will attempt to direct the therapy, often going as far as attempting to sabotage it.

This Destructive Relationship Syndrome pattern deteriorates into an ongoing, marathon therapy session. The couple's communication is more a therapeutic interaction, than a real conversation. The Therapist talks to the Significant Other as if she were a patient. Meanwhile, the Patient acts like a patient.

Here is a typical exchange between a couple who are locked into *Therapist/Patient*:

"You are in Denial just like your mother. You need to get in touch with your real fear. Why don't you admit that you won't go back to school because you have a deep unconscious fear of failing."

To this string of very inappropriate comments, she responds:

"You are right! I am afraid of failing. I can't help it. Do you really think I am like my mother? I hate that. I don't want to be like her. What should I do? Please help me. If you tell me what to do, I will do it."

The above is not from a specific case but it is typical of many transactions I have heard. This is a very destructive way for people to talk to each other. Many professional therapists have relationships based on this pattern. If both are therapists, they will often switch roles with the one who plays *Patient* suddenly becoming the *Therapist*. Sometimes, both want to play the same part simultaneously. Then, the real fun begins, if you call total chaos fun.

In a true therapeutic setting, all kinds of emotional cross currents are often set loose. The therapist may trigger anger, hate, fear, attraction and a host of other possibilities. These are all areas, which could possibly cause a problem. Each would need to be addressed. What do you do if your *therapist* is also your Significant Other?

One woman, who played the role of the Patient in a Therapist/Patient relationship, had this to say: "It's one thing to spill your guts to your therapist and another to have to get into bed with him!" She went on to say, "I never know if we are making love or if he is doing a clinical evaluation of me." This woman and her husband are psychologists and their marriage ended with a divorce. Neither was willing to settle for being a real person who was relating to another real person.

## The Teacher and the Pupil

The title of this pattern describes how this type of relationship is structured. In many situations, we could call this pattern, the *Parent* and the *Child*. Each person seeks a relationship based on the role he or she has learned to play. If it does become a Parent/Child pattern, the couple may also experience sexual difficulties. After all, it is uncomfortable to make love to someone who seems like your parent or your child.

In the Teacher/Pupil pattern, the pupil is always asking the Teacher what is the right thing to think or do. The Teacher will even attempt to *teach* the Pupil how to dress. Often the Teacher will even order the Pupil's food when they happen to be in a restaurant. I do not mean simply being courteous. The Teacher will tell the Pupil what to have and then place the order for the Pupil.

Another common trait of this pattern is for the Teacher to speak for the Pupil. Someone asks the Pupil for example, "I hear you are going to take some classes this year. What are you going to take?" To which the teacher responds while the Pupil looks on. Another response would be for the Pupil to ask the Teacher, "What should I take?"

As you can guess, these individuals are afraid they cannot be loved for just being themselves. Each has learned to manipulate in order to be *loved*. Also, they believe if they stop playing their role, they will no longer be loved. However, if the Teacher does a good job, the Pupil usually outgrows the relationship and leaves it. If the Teacher does not do a good job, the Pupil will find a better Teacher.

For the Teacher, the outlook is not any better. The Teacher will become angry and frustrated if the Pupil does not learn to the Teacher's satisfaction. Too often, the Teacher begins to denigrate the Pupil's abilities, habits or intelligence. When the Pupil still fails to perform to the Teacher's standards, the acrimony increases. The Teacher's next step is to begin looking for a more willing Pupil.

The Teacher/Pupil relationship is often filled with infidelity, as each person seeks out a better Teacher/Pupil. Occasionally, this Destructive Relationship Syndrome pattern escalates into abuse. This abuse is usually only verbal. Sometimes, it becomes physical. This pattern is always a very sad way for each to live and it seldom improves.

## The Sad Sack

With the Sad Sack pattern, one person has learned to be sad and depressed most of the time. A person learns the role of Sad Sack as a child. It occurs where he received attention and perhaps affection when he was sad. Sometimes, he may learn to be a Sad Sack by watching the pattern happen with someone else. No matter how he learns the pattern, the result will be the same. At least on an unconscious level, he will believe he can only be loved if he is sad.

The *Sad Sack* tends to have a very sad life style. Even if his life is really good, he will manage to see only the bad. Often the Sad Sack is fairly successful in several areas of his life. This makes him different from the Crutchie, the Lost Soul, the Patient or the Pupil. Because he may be successful at many things, other people often have trouble trying to understand why the Sad Sack is so sad.

I worked with one man who knew exactly what he was doing by being the Sad Sack. It did not matter what I did. He was unwilling to change this pattern. I still remember his words, "Why should I change. I can go into a bar, a singles event or Parents Without Partners and have some woman trying to mother me. She will take me home with her, feed me, give me sex and I don't have to do anything."

It is unusual for someone to have such a clear sense of what his pattern is. It is even more unusual that he did not want to change it. I still do not like what he stood for nor how he was playing on another person's weakness. However, I also feel sorry for him. He did not believe any woman could ever love or want him. So, he had to get what he could before they turned on him, which, in his mind, would be soon.

By now, I know you can make an educated guess as to just what DRS patterns he would appeal to. Also, I believe you are beginning to see how these patterns play off each other. This interplay contributes to finding painful, unhappy relationships.

## On the Rebound

This pattern may combine elements of any of the above patterns, with at least one addition: one of the players is required to just be ending or near ending another relationship. It is even better if the person who is on the rebound is coming out of a Destructive Relationship.

For example, the person on the rebound is in a violent, abusive relationship and is thinking about leaving it. At this point, in steps the Teacher or the Savior or the Crutch or the Therapist. Now we have a really good start on a painful relationship. With a little *luck*, this new couple will be in turmoil much faster then would be the case without a person On the Rebound.

Most psychologists agree it takes from six months to two years after ending a relationship, before we have closed that chapter in our lives. With some individuals, the time can be even longer. Anyway, if a person is in a deteriorating relationship or has just left one, there is no way he is ready for another relationship. His emotions are raw and he will be in a very confused state of mind. In spite of these things or perhaps because of them, some men and women are very *attracted* to someone who is On the Rebound.

I can only imagine one way to make On the Rebound a more exciting pattern. This is where both parties are meeting on the rebound. Wow! Now we have excitement. It is almost as if they are starting with four people in their new relationship: the two of them and their respective former Significant Others.

Each not only can find faults with the other, they can also watch for similarities and accuse the other of being just like . . . .

Of course, first they must get by the honeymoon stage, which usually lasts fewer than three months. Then it all starts again. All the unresolved conflicts and DRS patterns come roaring back. Only now, both parties are better at having failed relationships. Let us not even consider the children of these failed relationships. If we do, then things get very complicated.

## The Bully and the Victim

This Destructive Relationship Syndrome pattern requires special mention because it is truly dangerous. In this pattern we find one person, usually a woman, who seeks out and finds someone who will inflict abuse on her. While this abuse is usually verbal, too often, it also turns physical. If you suffer from either end of this pattern, the Bully or the Victim, I implore you to get professional help.

I have said I do not want this book to be about therapy. That is why I do not want to go into all the factors which make up this pattern. I do want to touch on a few to impress on you the importance of changing this pattern, if you are either part of this pattern.

The Bully has usually been abused while growing up. He has bought into: *This is how you keep them [women] in line.* The Bully feels a deep sense of inadequacy and lives in constant fear of being made to look bad. He keeps this fear inside, which leads to rage. Then, he explodes. Usually, he will attack the people closest to him. This will usually be his Significant Other and often his children too.

The Victim is someone who has been trained to believe everything is her fault. Therefore, she deserves to be abused. Usually, the Victim was abused as a child or saw parents being abusive. This abuse may have been physical, verbal, sexual and often, all three. Victims grow up believing that if they were better lovers, wives or . . ., their (usually) man would not need to abuse them. The Victim is also afraid that no one else, in the whole wide world would want or love her. In the Victim's mind, it is better to hold on to what she has.

The Victim also believes there is nothing that can be done to change the situation. To be the Victim is to assume the role of a helpless player in life. Usually, Victims are convinced they do not have the ability, power or smarts to change any important parts of their lives. Often, they have trouble accepting responsibility for any of their decisions or actions. This causes their situation to be even more difficult. "After all, if I cannot change it, I might as well accept it" is a refrain I have heard too often to count.

The above descriptions merely scratch the surface of the Bully and the Victim. Also, the Bully and the Victim always have painful, abusive relationships which are frightening to everyone involved. Victims often suffer from a complete lack of self-worth. Because of this, they will not take any steps to protect themselves.

The Bully lives in a state of constant terror and rage. This drives him to attempt to completely control the other person. He does this in a desperate effort to feel more powerful and better than at least one other person in his world.

This pattern can be changed but it is not easy. It takes commitment and time. If you find yourself in the role of either the Victim or the Bully, please talk to someone. You need professional help. At least talk to your Minister, Rabbi, Priest or a trusted friend. I believe sooner or later, you will need to see someone who is trained and experienced in dealing with these patterns. If you cannot do it for yourself, then do it for the sake of those whom you love.

## Wrapping It Up

It would make things easier for all of us, if everything and everybody acted in understandable, predictable and exact patterns. This is just not real life. When it comes to real people and Destructive Relationship Syndrome specifically, many combinations and nuances are possible and probable.

As you read about the different DRS disguises, you may have thought, "Well, I do some of that but not all of it." This may simply be because these patterns are not as cut and dried as I described them. It is common for someone to have parts of more than one DRS disguise. Sometimes, a person will have played both ends of the pattern.

The important thing to remember is this: These patterns all perpetuate Destructive Relationship Syndrome. The common denominators of these patterns and roles is that they are based on manipulation and control, with one person being *the top dog*. History shows that where a person or a group of people sets themselves to be better than other people, it is only a matter of time before there is a revolution. While revolutions may be necessary, they always cause pain.

## Points To Remember

1. Destructive Relationship Syndrome patterns come in many disguises. No matter what the disguise, the patterns make the possibility of a successful relationship nearly impossible.
2. The most common patterns are: The Crutch and the Crutchie; The Savior and the Lost Soul; The Therapist and the Patient; The Teacher and the Pupil; The Sad Sack and On the Rebound.
3. These patterns are often not clear-cut. A person may have parts of more than one. Also, a person may switch from one to another within a relationship. It is the consistent evidence of one or more of the patterns that matters.
4. The Bully and the Victim is a special combination. It can be fraught with danger. If you or your Significant Other fit either part, you need professional help.

## Chapter 5

# *Just a Little Insanity*

As you read the case examples I include in this book, you may find yourself reaching a decision. You may decide that many of these people seem to act Just a Little Insane. Yet, most of these individuals act quite sane in their everyday lives. It is only when they are in a relationship that something seems to happen to their minds. From time to time, I may call specific behavior or attitudes "insane" or "crazy." I want you to know I am not referring to a clinical condition.

I know it is important for me to define for you what I mean when I say, "Just a Little Insanity." One philosopher has said, "It is a form of insanity to continue to behave in the same manner while also demanding a new outcome." If you recall, a fundamental sign of DRS, is the recurring pattern of getting into situations which end painfully. Yet, most often, the person who does this truly believes he will achieve a different outcome - this time.

To the phrase, "Just a Little Insanity", I want to add another definition. I believe that an individual is acting "Just a Little Insane" when he continues to act in ways which have historically produced pain, while insisting this time it will be different. As you examine my case examples, your own experiences and the experiences of others, you will see how these often match this part of my definition.

Another philosopher, while debating the subject of crazy behavior, has also contributed to my definition of "Just a Little Insanity". This philosopher said, "A sane person will not knowingly act in ways which would cause him or his loved ones pain. He concluded, "If an individual did intentionally act so as to cause himself or loved ones pain, he was acting crazy." He based his position on a belief, widely accepted in psychological circles: Individuals nearly always act in their own *perceived* best interest.

Most of us attempt to act in ways we have come to believe will bring us a benefit. This is what I mean when I say, "A sane person will *seldom* knowingly act in ways which will cause pain to him or his loved ones."

Conversely, those who suffer from Destructive Relationship Syndrome often appear to go out of their way to get into painful situations. At a minimum, they cause themselves pain and often their actions help to cause pain for those whom they love. Their behavior violates my understanding of sane behavior.

If we accept the definitions I have listed, we can agree on what I mean by "Just a Little Insanity." This will lead us to conclude that when it comes to some relationships, people often act as if they are "Just a Little Insane." This form of insanity is the direct result of Destructive Relationship Syndrome.

## DRS and Insanity

You would be safe believing that if an individual suffers from Destructive Relationship Syndrome, she or he has a history of acting "Just a Little Insane." We all know someone who seems to end up with the same person, again and again. Just the names change. Their relationships always leave them sick and tired.

Sure, their last Significant Other was blond and this one has red hair, or one was slender while the other was fuller bodied. See – they really are not the same person. Bull! These are cosmetic differences, which are only superficial. They do not make a real difference.

One woman had incredibly bad luck. Somehow she continued to find herself in relationships with men who were alcoholics. She had twice been married to alcoholics and had other serious relationships with problem drinkers. Yet, she would not believe that continuing to become involved with alcoholics was a little crazy. Instead, she went to great lengths to prove her choices were reasonable. If we examine her behavior as it pertains to her relationships, it fits all three parts of our definition of "Just a Little Insanity".

When I pressed her for details about her latest relationship, it was as if she were living on another planet. Somehow, she was unaware of her boyfriend's destructive patterns. She would invent wonderful reasons to explain her increasingly odd behavior. For example, she had begun to write bad checks to cover his bad checks. Also, she ran up large charges on her credit cards to buy him things.

She was doing these things, while she was unable to pay her own bills. "After all, I am just showing him how much I care" was one reason she offered me as an explanation. I say she was acting "Just a Little Insane," at least by our definition.

## Jim – Rescues the Damsel

Jim was an engineer and very careful in most areas of his life. Yet, he somehow continued to find himself in painful relationships. If he met the *right one* [See Chapter 6, It Must Be Love] he would begin to act as if he had misplaced his mind. His last misadventure with a woman finally caused him to seek help. He met this woman in circumstances best described as "nuts."

This woman was living with Jim's neighbor. Often, this couple had knockdown – screaming matches. Jim had occasionally talked to this woman around the condo complex where they lived. Little by little, she began to confide in him about her misery. Jim began to give her advice and a shoulder to cry on. Soon, they were spending considerable time together. He was becoming increasingly involved in a situation which was really none of his business.

One night, Jim overheard a terrible fight between this lady and her boyfriend and Jim called the police. When the police came, they wrote a report and left. Jim's neighbor then punched Jim in the mouth. The woman got hysterical and ran into her condo where she swallowed some kind of pills. She said she was going to kill herself. Her boyfriend then threw her out.

Jim drove her to the emergency hospital, where it turned out she had overdosed on . . . **Antacids!** What was Jim's response to all this excitement? After a few days, he asked her to move in with him. [Have you discovered just which DRS in Disguise(s) is being acted out? See Chapter 4].

It took almost a whole week before the lady was again spending time with her boyfriend. Jim began to stay awake nights worrying about her and the situation. He stopped exercising and began to experience problems at work. He quickly became a wreck! As a bonus he also began to experience depression. "After everything I did for her, how could she do this to me?" he asked.

This was not the first time Jim had acted like the Lone Ranger – riding in to rescue a woman in distress. Often, he acted as if his main mission in life was to be a Crutch. So of course he needed to find someone who was broken. Then, he could hold them up. As you may remember from Chapter 4, DRS in Disguise, if a Crutch does its job, the Crutchie will not need it anymore. Then the Crutch gets thrown away. This was the story of Jim's relationship life!

If Jim's recurring pattern is not an example of acting "Just a Little Insane," then I am missing something. I am sure you can come up with many good examples on your own. You may find examples from your own history or perhaps from the histories of some of your friends. Each example will probably have at least one important thing in common. Each situation ended painfully.

## Recurring Insanity

One typical aspect of Destructive Relationship Syndrome is the *recurring* pattern of acting "Just a Little Insane". I do not mean the same little insanity each time. It means when it comes to relationships, there is "Just a Little Insanity" here, there and everywhere. Search your own history concerning your relationships. If you have found yourself getting involved with the same type of person as in previous painful relationships, it strongly suggests a history of Destructive Relationship Syndrome.

Another indicator is a history of relationships, which besides ending painfully, also had some craziness involved. Craziness can come in many forms. If you were once involved with an addictive person and another time with someone who was depressed and still another time with someone in the midst of a crisis, guess what? This is a recurring pattern. If you have picked several people who have rejected you, this too is a recurring pattern.

What do I mean by the same type of person? There are so many combinations, I can only give you several examples. You will need to use your imagination and perhaps, draw on your personal history. To do this, you will need to step back and look at your history, with a great deal of objectivity. Imagine you were someone else while you look at this history.

If you have found yourself involved with someone who had a good deal of anxiety and so have any of your previous Significant Others, it suggests a recurring pattern. Finding yourself attracted to, or getting involved with depressed people, is another possible red flag. One classical pattern is finding yourself in relationships with someone who either cannot hold a job or is unable to get anywhere in life.

I have already mentioned becoming involved with people who have drinking problems. If you have been involved with individuals who in one case did booze and in another did drugs and in another, was a compulsive gambler, you are finding the same person repeatedly. All these conditions are usually the same condition. Just the surface manifestations are different.

## A Little DRS

At the time of writing this book, I was working with a woman who had repeated her pattern at least seven times. She kept finding men whom shrinks would label as "Rigid Compulsive." In one relationship, the man told her how to dress, talk and act. He even began to buy her clothes for her. In her last relationship, she was involved with a man who was a workaholic and wanted everything in its place. Of course, its place was wherever he decided it belonged.

She brought him with her to one of our sessions. He arrived with a computer-generated list of what he had decided we should talk about. When I told him I did not work this way, he threatened to leave. While he stayed, he refused to contribute to the session. Within a few days, he had called me several times. He wanted to find out what was going on in our sessions.

I reminded him that my sessions with her were private and confidential. This did not stop him. He would attempt to report about her behavior, her progress, or what he considered her lack of the same. His goal was to control me and through me, her. It did not matter to him that his plan was not working. He persisted with this plan anyway.

I told him several more times that I was not at liberty to discuss these matters with him. Then, he blew his top. He told the woman she had to choose between him and that *"God Damned Son of a Bitch!"* She told him she would stop seeing me but did not bother telling me about this decision. Instead, she decided to continue seeing me, while lying to him, also to me. Of course, this blew up in all of our faces.

One man I worked with had twice married women who loved to flirt. They were extremely good looking and liked to dress sexily. He was raised in a small town and was almost a prude. In his mind, a *good* woman would stop *flaunting* it, once she got married. Of course, the women in question had other ideas.

Also, he had never bothered telling the women about this "Little Insanity." Before I forget, both marriages ended in divorce. When last I saw him, he was again involved with a *flashy* woman. This time she was still married. Also, she was not sure she wanted to leave her husband. These things did not even slow him down.

## More Insanity

Let me mention a few more examples of "Just a Little Insanity". How about the unfaithful pattern? This requires you to be having sex with someone who is already involved with someone else. Also, it helps if you have been in this kind of situation before. This is more than "Just a Little Insanity". It is destructive to everyone who is involved.

If you are the person who is in a relationship and *getting it on* with someone else, your relationship is in trouble. You have some issues, which you need to address personally. You are cheating yourself and the other people too. These things nearly always end badly for everyone.

Getting involved with someone who is just ending a relationship [See On the Rebound, DRS in Disguise, Chapter 4], is another form of "Just a Little Insanity". A person ending a relationship is usually in pain, a little lost and in a confused mental state. These are not the attributes one would like to have while attempting to build a relationship.

Another example is getting involved with someone whom you meet at recovery meetings, group therapy or . . ., where either of you is just beginning to attend.

Entering these kinds of programs requires a sense of purpose and commitment. Often, when you first begin these programs, you will find it stressful. It may take most of your energy to make the progress you want. You just do not have the energy, stability or calmness needed to begin a relationship.

Here is another pattern for you to consider. This pattern has you becoming involved with someone whose general life style and goals are very different from yours. You know this and you choose to ignore these differences. This is also a case of "Just a Little Insanity". In Chapter 10, I discuss in detail, just how important differences in life style goals can be to a relationship.

Keep in mind, I am not referring to one occurrence of the above patterns. I am asking you to consider if you have a pattern of involvement in these types of situations. Also remember, it does not have to be the same type of involvement. If you can see you seem to have a combination of the types of involvements I have mentioned, you need to consider some important changes.

## Home Work

Yes, it is that time again – time for you to do some work. What I would like you to do is to examine at least two of your important relationships. Three would be even better. Your purpose is to discover if there are certain similarities in the people with whom you have had serious relationships.

Take a sheet of paper and on one side, write out a list of the positive attributes one of your Significant Others had. Make the list as complete and honest as you can. There is no need to make this person out as better than he or she really was. Also, do not ignore this person's good points because you are angry with this person.

On the other side of the page, list this person's negative behavior and attributes. Be just as honest and objective on this part of your home work as you were on listing the positive attributes. If your S.O. had a drinking problem, list it. If this person was an emotional elevator, [up and down] say so. If your S.O. was chaotic, write this down. Be as complete and honest as you can be.

After you have completed your list on one of your Significant Others, take a break. After about thirty minutes, read what you have written and think about what you discover. Then put this list away for a few hours. You see, this assignment may stir up some discomfort for you.

After your break, repeat the assignment on another Significant Other. Again, it helps if you can do this assignment on three relationships, which were important to you. However, one relationship, which was really chaotic and unhappy, can teach you some very important and useful lessons.

Please do not just do this assignment in your head. There is something about writing things down which makes the information more meaningful. It also helps to make things more understandable. When you can look at all the factors and compare the good with the bad, you will more easily see any patterns which may exist in your life.

## Linda – the Jerk Finder

This case contains many of the aspects you have been reading about. As you read this case history, you will see all three parts, which make up my definition of "Just a Little Insanity". You will also find many factors I will discuss in Chapter 7 – the Warning Patterns.

Linda was brought up in a very unstable home which was filled with tension, fear, chaos and depression. Her father, a successful physician, was emotionally unstable and subject to long bouts of depression. These episodes were often interrupted by explosive outbursts of anger. While these hostile outbursts were usually directed at his wife, sometimes he directed them at Linda as well. His verbally abusive episodes often lasted for several days.

During these emotional outbursts, he would attack all women in general. He said women were stupid and good for only one thing. Occasionally, he directed similar remarks to his wife and less frequently toward Linda. There were some instances when he called his wife a stupid bitch or dumb broad in front of others. Linda remembered once where her father got so verbally abusive, her mother ran out of a restaurant crying. She took a cab and disappeared for two days.

When I first met Linda, she had just ended a very painful relationship. As we discussed this, it was clear to me, Linda had successfully recreated her childhood. Only now, she was playing her mother's part and the part of little Linda.

Her ex-boyfriend was given to extreme mood swings. He would stay depressed for many days. Often he would turn verbally abusive and call Linda stupid. He would correct her way of speaking, dressing or acting. Often, he did these things in front of other people, including Linda's friends.

While they were living together, he consistently threatened to leave Linda for someone "who has some brains and isn't such a baby." Sometimes he would disappear for several days. When he returned, it was obvious to her, he had been with another woman. On the few occasions Linda got up the courage to confront him about his running around on her, he would blame her. Linda would be accused of being worthless in bed, ugly and of course his stand by favorite, stupid.

This disturbed man also took the position that if he didn't spend some time with a woman who was his intellectual equal, he would become a mental midget like Linda. One day, he left Linda for good and moved in with another victim, whoops I mean another woman.

Although what I have described thus far is grim, it is only the introduction to this case of "Just a Little Insanity". It gets better or perhaps worse, depending on your viewpoint.

Linda had met Mr. Jerk while he was still living with another woman. While he was polite and charming to Linda initially, he made terrible comments about the woman he was living with. During one of their first dates, a waitress did something that displeased him. As she walked away, he called her a stupid bitch.

Linda ignored all the warning signs because, "he seemed to pay a lot of attention to me and acted as if I were important to him." She also let pass comments like, "Women should stay in their place and stay away from all that equality crap!"

In spite of all the signs of danger, Linda found reasons to keep seeing him. Soon she was having sex with him. Also, he was staying at her apartment most of the time. Meanwhile, he began to complain that Linda was a lousy lover. He would compare her with other women and his mood swings, which had always been present, escalated. Linda kept coming back for more and soon he moved in with her. This was the beginning of nearly two years of Hell for Linda.

Another part of this history is important and sad at the same time. This Jerk was the second Mr. Jerk in Linda's relatively young life. Before this Mr. Jerk, she had managed to get herself enmeshed with Jerk the First! Both situations were nearly carbon copies of each other. Each situation was also nearly identical to her parents' relationship.

The case of Linda really fits the description of "Just a Little Insanity". Linda is a bright, capable and attractive woman. She also handles her career well and her friends and co-workers think highly or her. Yet, whenever she meets *the Right One* something happens inside Linda. She begins to act a little crazy. That is what this chapter is about.

If you are someone with a history of unhappy relationships and perhaps suffer from Destructive Relationship Syndrome, then you have acted with "Just a Little Insanity". Until you make a firm commitment to change what you have been doing, you will continue to fall into the same traps. Your results will be more pain and unhappiness.

## Points To Remember

1. If your relationships fit the definition of Destructive Relationship Syndrome, you have been acting with "Just a Little Insanity"

2. It is the recurring nature of "Just a Little Insanity" that keeps people locked into their unhappy relationships.

3. Addiction is addiction and bad behavior is bad behavior. Even where your Significant Others had variations of addictions or bad behavior, it still means the same thing. You have been repeating your Little Insanity.

4. You need to examine two or three of your previous relationships. The goal is to find what patterns of "Just a Little Insanity" you may have engaged in. Then, you must be willing to work on changing your patterns.

## Chapter 6

# *Instant Love?*

He walked into the crowded room and began looking around. Of all the places he could be, he really did not want to be at this place. Not now – not ever. Parties always made him uncomfortable and he never knew what to say to people. He had resigned himself to standing around, making small talk with anyone he might know. Except for having a few drinks, he could look forward to wasting one more evening . . . and then it happened.

As he was looking around, he saw HER! His pulse began to do a dance accompanied by the rapid beating of his heart. His eyes locked on her until, all he could see was her. Her eyes held his and he knew she was looking right at him. He desperately wanted to walk over to her but his fear rooted him in place. He knew he had to meet her. She seemed to offer him a smile as if to encourage him. Right then, he knew he had to act before the moment was gone.

Slowly and very deliberately, he started across the room, closing the distance separating them. He wanted to move slowly so he could still have time to retreat. She continued to smile as she watched him. Encouraged by this, he continued moving toward her.

Soon they were deep in conversation. For each, the whole world had retreated. He was oblivious to anything but this woman and she seemed to be in that same special place. All he knew was, he had to get to know her; to be close to her and to see her again. He did not want to do or say anything, which would spoil this moment. This was definitely it - Love at First Sight!

They began dating. Soon, they were spending nearly all of their non-working time together. The feelings between them were always intense. Both seemed unable to get enough of the other. Still, they wanted more. Both knew they had found that one special person they had been searching for.

Within a few weeks they were, for all practical purposes, living together. They still had their own places but little by little, her personal things began to take up more space in his home. She only returned to her apartment to pick up mail and to go through the motions of checking on what had become, without her recognition, her former home.

Soon it was official. They were living together and she had moved all her possessions into his house. This was a giant step for both and they knew it. Yet their love was so strong, they were sure this was the right thing to do. Of course there was some strain because of the new situation.

Also, they had a few heated arguments. Both believed these things were supposed to happen when people were getting to really know each other. After all, what was important was their mutual attraction. They had experienced the magical chemistry called, Love at First Sight.

> "The advantage of love at first sight is that it delays a second sight." (Natalie Clifford Barney (1876-1972), U.S.-born French author. "Samples from Almost Illegible Notebooks," London, 1962).

## The Magic Fades

Within a few months, the magic was putting in fewer appearances. They were discovering just how many habits and behaviors each had which the other did not like. Each was now on a private and secret crusade to change the other. After all, since their feelings were so intense, this relationship had to work.

In spite of all their efforts, their disagreements began to take control of them and their relationship too. Each was becoming angrier with the other. Both thought that the other was not putting in enough of the *right kind of effort*. Both began to wonder how they had arrived in such a painful, tense and unhappy relationship, again.

Their downhill slide gathered speed. Within a short time, the only things they had left in common were bitterness and anger. After one fight, which topped all previous fights, they decided to end the relationship. She found a place of her own and moved out. Within a few days, both were miserable and they missed each other. After a few telephone conversations and two dates, they decided to try again.

This time, they would make the relationship work. What I call the Honeymoon phase, lasted just two days. After this, war was declared again and this time it was *take no prisoners*! When she left this time, they knew it was the last chapter of a bad book. Each was disappointed, angry and bitter. Of course, each blamed the other for everything which had happened to them.

# Instant Attraction

I am sure many of you can relate to the little romance novelette you have just read. If something like this has not happened to you, you may have friends who have experienced the thrill of Instant Attraction. They probably called it Love at First Sight. I am sad to say, Instant Attraction Relationships nearly always end badly. It is because these attractions are based on illusions.

John Keats (1795-1821), when discussing illusions, put it very well. He said, "It appears to me that almost any man may like the spider spin from his own innards his own airy citadel." (Published in Letters of John Keats, no. 48, ed. by Frederick Page, 1954).

When we allow our emotions to blind us and help create illusions, we are risking everything on Nature's whims. Being attracted to someone along with having good feelings toward them is important. However, good feelings and attraction are not enough, if you want to build lasting, successful relationships.

I believe Instant Attraction is often a form of temporary insanity. Because of the damage it often causes, I have made Instant Attraction a separate pattern of Destructive Relationship Syndrome. Instant Attraction could easily fit within the chapter on "Just a Little Insanity."

As I mentioned earlier, when we meet that *special person* we often go into a mental fog and our brain cells go on vacation. We may do things and agree with conditions, which when viewed from a position of sanity, prove we are a little demented.

Our feelings may become so intense, we will jump right into the situation. We may not even think twice about our leap of faith. While we may have a sense of danger, we ignore the warning. This is similar to jumping off the roof of a twenty-story building and as we fall we say, "Well, so far it's working. I guess everything will be OK." It seems true, at least until you hit the ground.

You would be justified in asking, "If Instant Attraction (Love at First Sight) is so bad, why does it happen?" Not only is this a good question, it is very important you have an answer. I will do my best to give you one, which can help solve the mystery of Love at First Sight.

## Defining Instant Attraction

Before I give you my impression of the cause of this condition, I have another confession to make. No one knows for sure what produces Instant Attraction and Love at First Sight. The answer I offer is not to be taken as scientifically valid nor as the final word from an expert. My answer simply makes common sense. It is based on the patterns I have seen in my private practice while using hypnosis for nearly thirty years.

Over many years of working with those who had been bitten by the "Love at First Sight" bug, I became aware of what to me, were interesting patterns. Also, the Instant Attraction virus seemed to contain specific characteristics. These characteristics and patterns, along with my observations, led me to the answer I will now offer to you.

Imagine you have felt Instant Attraction sometime in your past. You were totally focused on one *Special Person.* Yet, for all you knew, this person could have been Jack [or Jacqueline] the Ripper. The intense feelings you were experiencing cannot have anything to do with the person you were attracted to. After all, you do not even know how he votes or even if he votes. You do not even know if this person has a functioning brain!

Let us also imagine, this very intense attraction was based on many factors, which you were not even conscious of. We could say your Instant Attraction was the product of unconscious processes and responses. If this is true, you would not have any idea about what was responsible for your intense attraction.

What if the person's facial structure reminded you, unconsciously, of the first person you ever had a real crush on? Perhaps the hair color was like the hair color of the first boy or girl you ever *soul (tongue) kissed.* What if the eyes were similar to the eyes of the first person you ever did heavy petting with?

Perhaps the general body type was similar to that of the first person you went steady with. What if this person carried him or herself in nearly an identical way as the first person you ever made love to?

Wow! Imagine all these important and powerful emotional experiences, coming together at one moment in time. I think you can see how powerful our responses might be. Each experience I have mentioned would, by itself, leave a strong impression on your psyche. It is no wonder, if they all come together at once, it would feel as if it were "Love at First Sight."

Yet, not one experience I have described, as wonderful and powerful as it may be, had anything to do with the person you felt the Instant Attraction toward. Instead, you are responding to many pieces of your history. This is what I mean when I say it is all based on illusions.

If the person you were instantly attracted to, simply looked like a specific person from your past, you would probably know it. At least, you would probably soon figure out what was occurring. However, how could you expect to recognize all these separate experiences and people from your past? I do not think you can.

Perhaps you could sit with a pad and pencil and ask yourself many questions. "Of whom do those eyes remind me and whom have I dated who had the same skin tone? Let me see, whom did I date that had the same build or body type as this person? Which person from my past does this person's hair remind me of?" If you could answer these questions, you might figure out just where your feelings of Instant Attraction are coming from.

You and I know it is very unlikely that any one of us is going to take this kind of inventory. It is even less likely when individuals are caught up in the excitement of Instant Attraction. Even if they did take time to do this kind of inventory, they might still have trouble attempting to isolate all those events and people from their past. One thing makes this area so tricky. Most of the connections occur on an unconscious level.

## Mini-Hallucinations

There is an easier way to know what is happening to you. Starting now, just assume Instant Attraction and Love at First Sight are always based on your hallucinations! If you are standing too close to a fire, you will feel the heat. Do you use the feeling of heat as an invitation to jump into the fire to see how badly you can get burned? I hope your answer is a resounding no.

If your answer is no, why would you use the heat of an emotional fire as an invitation to jump in? If you do jump into a relationship, while in the grasp of Instant Attraction, you will often have an opportunity of finding out just how badly you can get burned.

Let me make one point clear. I am not saying you must or even should ignore your feelings of Instant Attraction. Of course if you are already in an ongoing relationship a different rule applies. You can allow yourself to experience these feelings for someone other then your Significant Other. Then, forget it! You cannot act on these feelings. Just smile to yourself and think, "Wow, this feels good." Now, go about your business.

In any other case, I strongly recommend you enjoy the feelings but proceed with caution. Since you now recognize these feelings are based on hallucinations, you know they have little to do with the target of your Instant Attraction. Take your time and find out what the person is really like. This will help you separate the reality of this person from your fantasies about this person. It will also help you to avoid being like the moth who flies into the flame and then discovers his mistake.

Actually, you want to be even more cautious than you might otherwise be, if you were not into such intense feelings. After all, being in a state of "Just a Little Insanity" is probably not the ideal time to be making important decisions. The exception would be if you really like the pain and do not mind continuing to have Destructive Relationship Syndrome.

## Two Patterns

In this chapter and the last, I introduced you to "Just a Little Insanity" and "Instant Love" These two patterns often trick people into relationships, which nearly always fail. Your knowledge of these two patterns will enable you to avoid the traps they set.

With your knowledge of these traps, it should be easier for you to avoid them. By avoiding them, you make it easier to learn how to create happy, successful relationships. Please keep in mind, "Just a Little Insanity" and Instant Love (Love at First Sight) are often found within Destructive Relationship Syndrome. By now, your goals should be: Freedom from Destructive Relationship Syndrome and creating successful, loving relationships.

## Points To Remember

1. Whether we call it Love at First Sight, or Instant Attraction, approach the situation as if it were a form of Temporary Insanity.
2. The intense feelings are usually, if not always, based on a form of hallucination. While it is fine to enjoy the feelings, do not take them as proof of anything.
3. Instant Attraction is, to me, a form of unconscious process and response. Because of this, it will be difficult for you to discover just where the feelings are coming from.
4. When in the grip of Instant Attraction, be more cautious then you would be normally. Use the feelings as a warning much as a yellow light is a signal to slow down.
5. Never enter a serious relationship based solely on Instant Attraction. Take your time and get to know the real person as compared to your fantasy.
6. If you are in a relationship, respect it. If you find yourself instantly attracted to a person other than your S. O., look - enjoy - feel good - but DO NOT TOUCH! As the signs in retail stores state, "If you break it, you must pay for it!"

Chapter 7

# *Warning Patterns*

By now, you have learned much about Destructive Relationship Syndrome. I have told you about a few of the lies we have all heard and just what DRS is. Also, I have taken you through some major areas you need to know about, such as Instant Attraction (Instant Love and Love First Sight) and "Just a Little Insanity." You have also learned that Destructive Relationship Syndrome can come in many disguises. I have described many conditions, which may often lead to the development of Destructive Relationship Syndrome.

Now I want you to understand the major patterns which suggest your relationships are controlled by DRS. There are twelve patterns you need to become familiar with. If you often engage in these patterns, you have the opportunity to change them. By changing your patterns, you will give yourself a good start on being free from Destructive Relationship Syndrome.

If your relationship is mired in some or several of the DRS patterns, you can help to change this. With your knowledge and your decision to disengage from these patterns, you will encourage your relationship to change. Either way, you are giving yourself a chance to have a healthier, happier relationship. You will also give yourself the gift of a better map you can begin to follow.

Following are twelve Destructive Relationship Syndrome Patterns. The more you understand these patterns, the easier it will be to break those which are of concern to you. Some of these patterns are fairly obvious. Let me warn you. A few of these patterns are subtle and sneaky. Often, you find yourself *slowly* slipping into them. Slowly or quickly, they will end up causing you pain.

## The Twelve Patterns of DRS

1. Focus on Problems:

   Within a very short time, the focus of the relationship shifts more toward *the solving of problems*, past, present and future.

2. Communication Scramble:

   One and often both individuals may rely on disguised and often confusing communication. There may be destructive communication, such as name calling, verbal assaults and insults.

3. Tension — Stress — Anxiety:

   Very quickly, at least one and usually both appear to suffer with a high degree of stress and anxiety. Also, it is common for one to begin to blame the other for his or her own stress.

4. Crises - A Way of Life:

   The relationship begins to drain more time and energy, just to keep it going. One fundamental indicator of DRS is the Crises Factor: the relationship is in crisis, has just survived another crisis, or is getting ready to have a new crisis.

5. Pleasure Decreases:

   As time passes, there is a significant reduction in the pleasurable aspects of the relationship. In place of the pleasurable aspects, there is an increasing level of emotional pain and upheaval.

6. Arguments Instead of Solutions:

   Often, arguments begin to dominate the couple's communication. The couple's efforts at discussing issues lead to more arguments. Sometimes, arguments lead to long periods of silence. This silence may last for several days.

7. Destructive Behavior:

   In many situations, there begins to be, or already is, substance abuse, or other destructive behavior.

8. Distrust Grows:

   One or both individuals begin to display a high degree of distrust for the words and actions of the other. This leads to *demand*s for proof about what he or she says.

9. Justification and Excuses:

   At least one and usually both find they need to justify and excuse their behavior, or the behavior of the other, to their friends and family.

10. Abuse Increases:

    Verbal and sometimes, physical abuse begins to escalate. The increase in the behavior of verbal and physical abuse is significant. It indicates the relationship is moving into a dangerous condition.

11. Less Time for Constructive Pursuits:

    Often, the problems within the relationship consume whatever time is available. This leaves too little time or energy for pursuing productive, pleasurable and constructive activities.

12. Recurring Patterns:

    There is nearly always, a recurring pattern of any of the above. The recurring nature of these patterns produces essentially the same results: An unhappy, failed relationship.

## Self-Evaluation One

Now, comes a very important step. You need to do this self-evaluation. No one will be looking over your shoulder and no one will be second guessing you. Also, no one is going to criticize you. Allow yourself to be as honest as you can be. Take a sheet of paper and do a self-check list. Focus on one relationship. If you are in one and you are concerned about it, do the best you can to focus on this relationship.

If you are not in a relationship now, pick a previous relationship, which ended badly for you. I know this can be uncomfortable. Sometimes, a little discomfort now can help us avoid much more pain later. Looking back at your history gives you a chance to change your present and your future.

Start with the general definition of Destructive Relationship Syndrome: *A recurring pattern of seeking and/or finding individuals with whom, in spite of initial attraction and appearance, you are truly not compatible and with whom your relationship is problem filled. There are crises, arguments, generalized chaos, poor communication, and often verbal and sometimes physical abuse.*

If the definition is more true for you than not, admit it. Write out a statement on your work sheet. It might say something like this: "My relationships seem to fit the definition of Destructive Relationship Syndrome." or "I often end up with people who do leave me exhausted and unhappy. I may suffer from DRS."

Next, go through the twelve patterns one at a time. Write out each of the twelve as if they were a question. For example, look at pattern five: Did my last [or does my present] relationship begin to demand more time and energy just to keep it going? To the best of your ability, give an honest answer.

Avoid giving a simple yes or no answer. Expand your answer a little. As an example, for your answer to question five, you might write, "Often, I found myself so busy just trying to keep my relationship from sinking, I had no time for my best friends or even my family."

After going through the twelve patterns, you will have a very good profile describing which DRS patterns affect (infect?) you and your relationships. You will also have a good profile of your relationship(s). If this profile suggests you do indeed suffer from DRS, do not despair. Because you are being honest, you are giving yourself a chance to move onto the path of change. It is only when an individual acknowledges a problem that he or she begins the process of resolving the problem.

## Denial and Avoidance

Two of the most destructive attributes individuals can hold on to are, Denial and Avoidance. With denial, nothing can change. When a person is in denial, he does not even admit there is a problem. How do you fix what you will not admit exists? If you have relied on denial in the past, find a way to become honest with yourself. Unless you do, things will probably stay the same for you.

Typically, breaking through denial is the first major step to healing. It often leads to solutions. By doing the Self-Evaluation One, as honestly as you can, you are breaking out of denial. I want you to give yourself a pat on the back. You deserve it.

The second attribute I am asking you to avoid is avoidance! If an individual specializes in avoidance, he might admit to having the problem. He just will not do anything to change the problem. Instead, most of his energy goes to trying to avoid dealing with any part of the problem that might cause him discomfort. In his mind, dealing with problems causes pain – so avoid them.

One sad result of avoidance is that it usually produces even more pain. It may be uncomfortable to confront problems head on. It is much more painful to allow problems to grow into emotional cancer. While a person engages in avoidance, he is allowing problems to continue to grow.

Your self-evaluation will help you to go beyond Denial and Avoidance. It will also give you valuable information. This information will often give you the outline of the solutions you need. Armed with this information, you will be ready to take advantage of the techniques and processes which you will find through out this book.

Remember, it took many years of practicing DRS for you to end up with relationships which have made you unhappy and exhausted. It will take you some time and effort to break free of your patterns which have led you to such unhappy results. Please believe me - the results will make your efforts worthwhile.

## Herb and Sylvia – The Date

Before starting your self-evaluation, I want to describe another case to you. After you finish your self-evaluation, come back to this case and review it. By then, you will have a clear idea about the factors found in the DRS outline, which are present in this case. At the outset, let me tell you this is not a case I had anything to do with. I based this case on something presented on a major television network show. This program contained a segment about relationships.

One primary focus of this program was about how hard it is to meet someone to relate to. To illustrate this aspect, the program followed two people on their first date. The stated purpose was to show how they related to each other while on their first date.

Sylvia is a successful business woman. She had worked her way to a position of authority with her employer. She spends a good deal of money on clothes and likes to keep up with the latest in styles. Sylvia is also a strong supporter of what are called women's issues. Also, she believes women should have their own careers.

During the show, she said it was important for a man to be sensitive to the needs of any woman who wants to have a career. She said a woman's career should have the same priorities as a man's career. Another point she made, was that she believes in monogamous relationships. Her view was clear: A couple should be committed to each other – exclusively.

Herb owns a small, modestly successful business. Early in the show, he said he believed in the man making the decisions in a relationship. He said the woman should always accept and support the decision, once the man has made it. Also, he believed women should take a secondary role to that of a man in nearly every situation. During his interview he made several derogatory remarks about women's issues.

Herb was very interested in music. He expressed very definite ideas about what he considered to be artistically acceptable. He expressed a liking for romantic evenings and for love making in general. Later in the program he said men have a genetic predisposition toward needing and having many sexual partners. His position was that women must accept this and expect that men will stray.

According to Sylvia, Herb had arranged a very romantic evening for their first date. This date was filled with some very creative aspects. However, within a short time they had begun to argue about several issues. One of these was his adamant belief men should be free to pursue other sexual relationships. This, according to him, is true even if a man is married. Sylvia strongly disagreed and the discussion deteriorated into a heated argument.

Both knew they were being filmed during this date. There were cameras and people from the program all around. They could be assumed to have been on their best behavior. This leads me to wonder what their worst behavior might be like – but I digress.

They continued to argue, not only about the sexual issue but about women's issues in general. The volume of their conversation began to climb. Both evidenced a great deal of distress, which could be clearly seen on the film of their meeting. Because the camera was present, they tried hard to control their tempers. To this end, they had only a modicum of success.

After more time had gone by, Herb accused Sylvia of being "one of those women who emasculates men." Sylvia, while trying to control her anger, accused Herb of being a male chauvinist pig. She just used nicer language. Their arguments covered many areas and consumed about 75% of their time together.

During the lulls in their arguing, they discovered they liked the same kind of music. Herb was extremely knowledgeable about one specific musical instrument, which he played well. Sylvia also had knowledge and appreciation of the same instrument. After dinner, they adjourned, so that Herb could display his musical skills. Both enjoyed this interlude. It was the only activity which did not include any disagreement.

At the end of the evening, they were interviewed about their date. Responding to questions by the show's host, Sylvia said she would very much like to see Herb again. She said she would be upset if she did not have an opportunity to see him again. Herb said he would also like to *pursue the situation further*.

Sylvia and Herb agreed they would like to go out with each other again. Before the next date took place, Herb had jumped into a relationship with another woman. As an interesting aside, this woman originally did not want anything to do with Herb. "We argued too much," she said.

When Sylvia was told of this development, she was very upset. In spite of his new relationship, Sylvia said she still hoped to see Herb again. She thought that if they just got together to talk, they could work out their differences!

(**Cartoon in local paper**: [Man] "You don't want to be with me. I am unreliable, have a very bad temper and I don't want to be faithful." [Woman] "It doesn't matter. We would change all that if we got married.")

You now have more information about Sylvia and Herb then you probably ever wanted to know. At this time, do not do anything about it. Instead, go back and review the Twelve Patterns of DRS. After this review, complete your self-evaluation. When you finish, return to the case of Sylvia and Herb.

I know you will be pleasantly surprised at how many DRS factors you can now identify. Many patterns will probably jump out and grab you. Some patterns will require more effort to identify. By all means, do not ignore "Just a Little Insanity," since it fits Sylvia and Herb so well. Of course Sylvia and Herb may be "Just a Lot of Insanity."

With the completion of your self-evaluation, you have begun moving from understanding the problems to finding the solutions. If you are in a relationship, you can take steps to change any prevailing DRS patterns, which may be present. I have seen couples, at the brink of disaster, who turned their relationship into a happy, loving and respectful relationship. This happened when one or both made a concerted effort to change their own Destructive Relationship Syndrome patterns.

I have watched unattached people make dramatic changes in their lives, by changing the patterns, which have caused so much pain. These people find themselves interacting with others on an entirely different and healthier level. This has spilled over into their dating lives and has led them to find someone who was free of DRS. Before you ask, yes, they are out there.

I cannot stress too strongly the importance of doing your DRS Self-Evaluation One. Unless you like to swim in shark-infested waters, or enjoy diving into a swimming pool without water, your self-evaluation will be very valuable to you. For those who enjoy taking the risks I have just mentioned, pretend you have not read this chapter. After all, if everyone used good sense and had a good map, all the therapists would be out of business.

## Points To Remember

1. There are Twelve Patterns, which suggest the presence of Destructive Relationship Syndrome.
2. To be inflicted with DRS does not require that all Twelve Patterns be present. It is enough if several patterns are present.
3. By completing Self-Evaluation One, you will have a clear idea about your patterns and the patterns of your previous relationships.
4. It is important for your journey to succeed, that you go beyond Denial and Avoidance. Self-Evaluation One will help you do this.
5. Changing your DRS patterns can produce dramatic, positive changes for you and for your relationships.

CHAPTER 8

# *DRS or Not*

At this juncture, I have introduced you to nearly every component, which makes up what I call Destructive Relationship Syndrome. Now, I would like to introduce you to most of the symptoms and signs, which strongly suggests you or someone you know, may be suffering from the effects of Destructive Relationship Syndrome.

In earlier chapters, I touched on some of what you will be reading. Most of the material will be new and will help round out your understanding of Destructive Relationship Syndrome. I will also make some direct comparisons between individuals and couples who suffer from DRS and those individuals and couples who do not.

## Too Fast on the Draw

In the Old West, being fast on the draw may have been useful, at least in some situations. However, when it comes to relationships, being fast on the draw will nearly always get you into trouble. Entering a significant relationship much too quickly is, perhaps, one of the most common symptoms of DRS. Most often, this quickness sets the stage for disaster.

Those who suffer with Destructive Relationship Syndrome often find it almost unbearable to be out of a relationship. Their need to be with someone becomes so powerful, they neither stop, look nor listen before acting. Instead, when they meet someone who stirs up familiar feelings of attraction, they just jump in. This is just one more way to jump out of an airplane without a parachute.

Individuals who are free of DRS might also prefer to be in a relationship. However, they take their time finding someone they want to be with. They take even more time discovering if that person is someone who is really in their best interest. Most of these healthy people have a good amount of self-esteem. They enjoy their own company, life style and the activities they are involved in. They are not in a hurry to trade in what works for a life full of problems.

Sometimes, individuals who suffer from DRS will manage to stay out of a relationship for a reasonable period. At first glance, this behavior looks like the behavior of a DRS free person. On closer inspection, there are some important differences. People suffering from DRS usually stay out of a relationship because they are afraid of being rejected or hurt. They avoid dating or getting involved because history tells them what happens when they do meet someone they care about.

Also, when DRS individuals take a holiday from being involved with someone, it is usually because their last breakup left them too exhausted and hurt. Often, their lives are in chaos too. This leads them to resolve to straighten out their lives. To do this, they know they must avoid the temptations of another relationship. So they do, at least for a while.

Some individuals with DRS do very well as long as they stay out of an intimate relationship. They may even have a history of avoiding relationships for long periods. In my experience, their histories will show that their problems begin, as soon as they get involved with someone. This is when their pattern of DRS takes over and their lives then begin to grow chaotic.

It is only a matter of time before their new relationships are also chaotic. They quickly allow their new relationships to take over their whole life. It is as if a relationship is a big, dry sponge and they are just liquid, waiting to be sucked up.

The healthier DRS free individuals fight like Hell to not let their lives become disrupted by any relationship. Usually, these individuals feel good about themselves and their lives. Because of this, they want their relationships to complement their lives. They do not want them to take their lives over. They make sure to set boundaries, first for themselves, their Significant Others and for their relationships.

These healthy individuals have discovered the importance of keeping any relationship from becoming their whole life. On the contrary, they keep their relationships as a part of their life, although an important part. They insist their relationships fit into their complete lifestyle and not the other way around.

I tell people to view life as if it were a beautiful painting – a masterpiece. This painting should be filled with color, interesting shapes and textures. A relationship is an important part of a painting. It is not the whole painting. Whenever I have looked at those whose relationships are solid, loving and happy, this is how their relationships are. These people do not allow a relationship to obliterate the rest of their painting.

# Obsession

Another typical symptom of DRS, is obsessing. Nearly every person whom I have worked with, who suffers with DRS, has specialized in obsessing. These people obsess about their Significant Others and the condition of their relationships. The striking part of this obsession is the expectation of catastrophe. When all is going well, these individuals obsess about such things as: "How long will the relationship last? Will he get tired of me? When will he find someone else? What is he doing when I am not with him?"

Of course, if things should be going badly, it leads to a new and fertile field for her obsessions. She can obsess about all the possible causes of every problem she has. Also, about the problems she imagines will happen next. As her obsession intensifies, which it generally will, she will have less time for friends, hobbies and activities.

Often, her career suffers as well. This is due to the new career she has found for herself: Full Time Obsessor. She spends her time either preparing for future problems or is trying to save her relationship. Nothing else matters. Soon, she may even find herself obsessing about her obsessing. Often, this causes her to become compulsive about her Significant Other and the relationship itself.

> "It is only when we no longer compulsively need someone that we can have a real relationship with them." (Anthony Storr, British Psychiatrist and Author. The Integrity of the Personality).

While most of us give thought to our loved ones and our relationship, there is balance. Individuals and couples who are DRS free, usually keep their focus on the present. They focus on what is happening in the reality of their lives, individually and as a couple. When they are with their Significant Other, nearly the whole of their attention is with that person.

When they are at work, their attention is on work. If they are playing tennis, this is what they focus on. These individuals have discovered how to switch their attention as circumstances warrant. This suggests they maintain flexibility in what interest them.

Let me put it simply. Individuals who have a healthy sense of themselves and their relationships, are too busy with living to have time for obsessing. Conversely, those mired in Destructive Relationship Syndrome are too busy with DRS to have time for living. In Chapter 11, you will find what I not so humbly call, The Question of the Year. This question will help you to know just which camp you fit into.

## Louise – Bewitched and Besotted

Louise had a history of stormy relationships, which often turned very destructive. Within two or three dates, she would find herself in a relationship with a man she had just met. Often, the men she wanted were still in a relationship. Sometimes, they were in the process of ending a relationship or had just ended a relationship. None of these conditions (warning signs) influenced her one bit.

After one date with a man she was attracted to, she would begin to obsess about him. She would lay awake at night and wonder about things such as: "I hope he liked me. Maybe he won't call. Does he think I'm pretty? I hope I didn't sound stupid." She would also begin to rehearse exactly what she would say if he did call. Also, she would even begin to plan how and when they would go to bed together. Her obsessions would soon spill over into her daily life as well.

It is normal to do some wondering about what others think about us. Most of us might devote some time to this wondering. What sets Louise apart is the exaggerated degree of her wondering along with her inability to stop. Not only did her wondering (obsessing) begin to keep her awake at night, it would intrude in her daily thoughts and influence her work. She would also become anxiety ridden to the point of developing physical symptoms.

After a few dates, Louise might begin to spy on her new boyfriend. She would resort to this whether the relationship was working or not. Louise would drive by his house to see if he were with another woman. If he were not home, she would wonder where he was and become even more anxious. If the relationship continued, she would become more obsessed about what he might be doing, who he was with and what he really thought about her.

By now, her anxiety levels would be intense and she would begin to suffer with panic attacks. These attacks would prevent her from working, engaging in her hobbies or seeing her friends. With all this extra time on her hands, she could now obsess even more.

Louise would begin to *bug* the man in a desperate attempt to get him to reassure her about all her fears. If he did, this would give her temporary relief. Then, her obsessions would come roaring back and so would her anxiety. She would try to get more reassurance, which would again give her temporary relief.

Within a short time, she would begin to obsess again. Now she would obsess about if he were telling her the truth or hiding something from her. This would lead her to bug him some more until - *Another Breakup*. Just another notch on her belt of insecurity, failure and DRS.

Louise is perhaps an extreme example of obsessing about a relationship and a Significant Other. Still, there is much to learn from her pattern of obsession. When an individual is subject to obsessing, it is nearly impossible for them to ever have a successful relationship. Not only will people who obsess drive themselves crazy, their obsessing almost always drives other people away.

## Withdrawal Symptoms

Individuals who suffer from DRS, will experience withdrawal symptoms whenever they are kept from their Significant Others for even a short time. For example, I worked with one woman who experienced headaches, dizziness and depression whenever her husband traveled. She had a morbid fear someone would hurt her, because she was alone. Her withdrawal symptoms would become so painful that she would feel compelled to telephone him for reassurance.

It was common for her to call him ten or more times a day. Her goal was to get his reassurance he loved her and that everything would be OK. No matter how much he tried to reassure her, within a half hour of talking to him, her symptoms of withdrawal would come roaring back. This caused her to call again.

As she said, "All I could think of was that he wasn't here to take care of me. I was afraid he was with someone else." She also felt physical symptoms, which reminded her of when she had quit smoking a few years earlier. Anyone who has quit smoking (or has broken free of any addiction), will easily recognize what this woman was experiencing.

The severity of an individual's withdrawal symptoms is dependant on several factors: The length of the separation, how bad the individual's DRS is and what kind of tolerance for discomfort he or she has. Individuals may experience any one or more of the following symptoms of withdrawal:

1. Sleep problems, which can include: difficulty falling asleep, maintaining sleep or early morning awakening.
2. Intense anxiety that seldom recedes and often flares to new heights.
3. A general state of agitation.
4. Becoming emotionally super sensitive, easily upset or discouraged.
5. Impaired concentration.
6. Giving into or starting bad habits: smoking, drugs, excessive drinking.
7. Feelings of depression or sadness without any valid reason.
8. Violating one's personal code of ethics and conduct and justifying the behavior as necessary.

You should recognize, that under the right circumstances, anyone can experience some of the above withdrawal symptoms. If a long standing relationship ends, or a spouse dies, anyone might temporarily fall into one or more of these behaviors. However, without DRS, this will be only for a short time. Then the person will quickly do something to get back on track.

Individuals who are free of DRS, also miss a loved one when circumstances require they be apart. After all, if you love someone, you usually want to be with this person. However, during a separation the healthy person's life goes on, fully and in a generally satisfying fashion. These individuals have enough inner resources and external interests to fill the temporary gap in their lives.

Also, DRS free people have many interests, hobbies and friends they enjoy. While they will miss their Significant Others, they continue with their productive activities and with their friends. Because they are focused on living, they seldom experience the kinds of withdrawal symptoms I have outlined. If they do, the symptoms are usually mild and of short duration.

In a DRS situation, individuals have trouble getting past any or all of the above eight withdrawal symptoms. They also fall into them with very little reason. I would say an individual who suffers with DRS is like a loaded gun. He is just waiting to be fired. It just takes a little squeeze and the problems begin. I have worked with people who have started to show some withdrawal symptoms after just two dates. Why? Their date had not called to ask them for another date.

## Positively Negative

Often, individuals who suffer with DRS also have a primary focus on what is wrong or could go wrong. This leads them to only expect the worst. They also talk to everyone who will listen, about problems that are real, expected or merely imagined. They seldom talk about what is going well or things that are positive.

Being around them for any length of time can be very tiring and unsettling. This frequently drives healthy people away. As a result, these negative people often end up in relationships with others who share their dim view of the world. Then, it becomes a consistent marathon of negativity. When this happens, it reinforces the idea that the world is bad place.

In my opinion, these individuals believe it is problems, which bring and keep people together. Also, they are so focused on what is wrong, they usually overlook or depreciate everything that is going well. This attitude affects their lives in many ways. It can and usually will poison the atmosphere of all their relationships, intimate, professional and social.

When I examine successful, happy individuals and couples, I find the exact opposite attitude from those of DRS individuals. While these healthier individuals are not blind to problems, they are optimistic and put most of their attention on what is going well. As a result, their interactions with their Significant Others are most often positive in tone and affect. This attitude attracts others who also have a positive outlook.

DRS couples nearly always focus on and fight about what each perceives as wrong. When I ask a couple to put a moratorium on their fighting, I nearly always hear the same refrain. "How will we ever solve our problems if we don't keep talking about them?" This, in spite of the fact they have been fighting for most of the time they have been together and things have only become worse. Yet, they do not want to admit that their focus on problems may be a major source of their problems.

People who have good, healthy relationships, are solutions oriented instead of problem oriented. These people will attempt to identify a problem *quickly*. There is little blaming or histrionics. Their next step is to focus on finding possible solutions. They understand that finding a solution is what will improve the situation. This is almost exactly opposite of how a Destructive Relationship Couple will go about handling any problem.

Later, I will present the results of a study, which supports my contentions about negativity. For now, it is enough to say this study shows one important finding. Couples who focus on positive aspects, have a far higher chance of having successful relationships, than those couples who focus on problems and what is wrong. Those individuals and couples who focus on what is wrong are far more likely to have relationships that fail and are very painful for everyone.

## Not Me!

Individuals who have a pattern of focusing on negatives, are often unaware of just how negative they are. They may find this pattern to be objectionable in others. Yet, they continue to find only the fertilizer in a garden while overlooking all the flowers. Where a couple suffers from a pattern of negativity, it is almost overwhelming for everyone concerned. If either one or both are unaware of their patterns, it really complicates the situation.

In my office, I tape recorded a woman who was a champion of negativity. What I found interesting was her insistence that she was a very *up, positive person*. After I recorded her, I played the tape back while she listened intently. At one point, she frowned, looked at me and said, "I didn't say that!" To her credit, she began to laugh and said, "I can't believe I just denied my own voice."

Because individuals and couples who function under the cloud of DRS are often unaware of their negativity, I often approach this problem first. I know it is important for them to recognize their patterns of negativity. To help accomplish this, I ask these couples to record a few typical conversations. Also, I suggest they record one or two of their arguments.

When they carry out this assignment, they are usually surprised to discover just how busy they are promoting what is wrong. Often, the tape will be filled with each taking turns blaming and attacking the other. The thrust of their conversations are nearly always focused on problems, disagreements and who is at fault. What I often do not hear is any real effort to make anything better.

## The Anxiety Factor

If anxiety, which I call future dread, appears early in a relationship, it is a good indicator that something is wrong. While most individuals who suffer DRS tend to be anxious in general, a new Significant Other or entering a relationship is like raw meat to a hungry lion. There are only two reasons for anxiety to rear its head in a new relationship: there is something fundamentally wrong with the relationship or someone suffers from DRS.

Finding a special person or beginning a new relationship should be a time of great excitement, happiness and discovery. This is just what it is for healthy, DRS free individuals. For those who suffer with DRS, one of their main experiences is anxiety.

You should keep in mind that anxiety is often a warning. It is one symptom, which shouts out to be heard. If you or the other person experiences anxiety when beginning a relationship, pay attention. Either the relationship or the Significant Other is fraught with danger, or the anxious individual is suffering from Destructive Relationship Syndrome.

It may be argued that some anxiety is normal in some situations. However, the anxiety suffered by individuals with DRS is a sign something is wrong. If we accept anxiety as a form of future dread, then what is it the individuals expect in the future? It cannot be happy, successful lives. On the contrary, they must expect a disaster. Anyhow, beginning a relationship or meeting a special person is not supposed to be an invitation to become anxious.

Often, the Anxiety Factor and Obsessing are like twins, which go everywhere together. The more anxious DRS individuals become, the more they may begin to obsess. As they obsess, they will cause themselves to become even more anxious. It is a vicious cycle. If the cycle is not changed, it will only lead to pain, unhappiness and a difficult life. Until these DRS individuals learn how to go past anxiety, their lives will be filled with problems. If left unchecked, anxiety will undermine all sense of well being and competence.

## The Elevator Factor

In my practice, I sometimes tell an individual he is suffering from the *Otis Factor*. Most often he will respond by staring and then asking: "What is that?" I say, "Otis used to be the world's largest maker of elevators and elevators spend their entire lives just going up and down." The nicer individuals usually smile. Others may glare . . . but they, too, get the point.

Going from extreme highs to extreme lows, in the extreme [pardon the play on words] is called Manic-Depressive Disorder or Bipolar Disorder. I am not talking about this condition, which should be treated by a competent professional. This condition, which is far more serious then the Otis Factor, will usually prevent an individual from having a productive life, until this is treated.

I am talking about the tendency of DRS individuals to get almost euphoric when meeting Mister or Miss (and sometimes Mrs.) Right. Because this high is so strong, they often have no time for work, family or friends. Then the moment anything goes wrong or even not as right as wanted, boom! They get down, feel defeated and often engage in self-pity. Thus, the *Otis Factor*. Up one minute and down the next. This, like the anxiety pattern, is a reliable marker for the presence of Destructive Relationship Syndrome.

When we compare the *Otis Factor* with what is found in DRS free individuals, the contrast is illuminating. These healthy individuals are also happy when they meet someone special. The same is true when they enter a new relationship. They may even have a degree of euphoria but they do not allow it to bring their lives to a stand still. While they adjust to fit their new situation, they stay fully engaged in their lives. They make sure they still have time for family, friends, work and hobbies.

If something goes wrong they also will feel upset and will want to get rid of the problem. However, they will not allow the problem or their feelings to take over their lives. They do not *hit bottom* merely because something went wrong. This is to say, healthy individuals also go through mood changes. But they neither go through the roof on the way up nor into the basement on the way down. Their feelings are part of their experiences and not their total experience.

## A General Map

While I am sure I could write about more symptoms of Destructive Relationship Syndrome, I think you have enough to make an informed decision. Your first decision should be about yourself. After all, you will be living with you no matter what may or may not happen with your relationships.

I recommend you take time to think about what happens to you when you meet someone special or when you are in a relationship. If any of the symptoms I have discussed, pop up in your life, you need to acknowledge you may suffer from DRS. You can also decide if your symptoms played some part in the chaos of a relationship or in the ending of a relationship.

Your next decision may be a little more difficult. You need to look at your Significant Other or if you are not in a relationship, a past S.O. and determine if s/he evidences or evidenced DRS. In Chapter 7, you learned about the Twelve Patterns, which suggest when a relationship itself is probably based on Destructive Relationship Syndrome. You might want to take a few minutes and review those patterns. With your knowledge of these patterns and what you have read about the symptoms of DRS, you are well prepared to make this decision.

While knowing the truth may temporarily upset you, it will also give you a chance to change things. After all, if you are standing too close to a fire, you will feel the heat. That heat gives you the opportunity to move before you get burned. What you discover can be the heat that keeps you from getting burned again.

## Points To Remember

1. The faster you recognize the symptoms, which suggest DRS, the sooner you can act to negate their effects.

2. Some of the symptoms are: Too Fast on the Draw, Obsessing (about the relationship or the other person), Suffering from Withdrawal when you are apart, even for a short time, Negativity (A primary focus on problems and what can go wrong), Anxiety when meeting someone or starting a relationship, the Elevator Factor (Emotional highs when things go well, followed by lows when something goes wrong).

3. Decide what happens to you when you first meet someone special or when you begin a relationship. Do you experience any of the symptoms? Did these symptoms impact on your relationship?

4. You will need to make the same decision about your present or past Significant Other.

5. Knowing the truth about these patterns, will make it easier for you to change them.

CHAPTER 9

# *What's the Score?*

In Chapter 8, I asked you to uncover any potential which you may have for Destructive Relationship Syndrome. The DRS evaluation focused on the patterns found within Destructive Relationship Syndrome itself. Now, I want to introduce you to DRS: Scale Two. With this scale, you have the opportunity to rate yourself and any Significant Other about the potential for having a successful relationship.

DRS: Scale Two contains twenty questions. These questions will help you recognize those traits, which bode well for a successful relationship. It will also help you see just which areas should be of concern to you. Sometimes, what you uncover about yourself or another person, can upset you. However, DRS: Scale Two can help you to have a solid sense of what may be causing problems for you, your relationships, or your Significant Other.

Again, it is important for your journey to be as honest and accurate as possible. When doing this evaluation, take time to consider your answers. By detecting your problem areas, you give yourself the chance to begin making important changes. Also, by discovering the areas of strengths and weaknesses your Significant Other has, you can probably know what is the real potential for a successful relationship with this person.

## Sally - Scale of Success

Let me tell you a success story concerning DRS: Scale Two. A woman I will call Sally, had a history of failed, painful and unhappy relationships. She had suffered with many of the DRS patterns you found in Chapter 7. Sally kept *falling* into bad situations without any idea of how this continued to happen.

As Sally's latest relationship was about to go up in smoke, she was referred to me. I helped her to end this abusive relationship and to become a more relaxed and calmer person. During her third session, I gave her my DRS: Scale Two to study. She looked at it and said, "No wonder we were so miserable. According to this, there never was a chance for us to make it."

Several months later, Sally called me with her success story. She had met a man and was attracted to him. Along with other things she had learned, she decided to evaluate him according to DRS: Scale Two. Sally was shocked by what she discovered. According to the DRS: Scale Two, this guy was a very poor prospect for a successful relationship. She decided she should slow things down. Instead of jumping in, she stepped back and watched the way he acted and handled situations in his everyday world.

Soon, she saw patterns suggesting that he was not a very nice person. He was verbally abusive with people he considered unimportant or beneath him. His list of people who fit this category was extensive. He acted as if all waitresses and waiters deserved to be mistreated. If he did not believe someone could benefit him, he was apt to become sarcastic toward him or her.

Sally's friends did not appear to warm up to him. When she asked them about this, they did not have any specific problems with him. One of her friends said, "It is just a feeling I get when I am around him. He makes me nervous." Also, she discovered he was not very flexible. When he did not get his way, he would pout. There were other areas which concerned her too.

While Sally was still in her observing phase, he jumped into a relationship with a woman he barely knew. Within a few weeks, he was cheating on this woman and was verbally abusive to her.

He was also given to storming out of their apartment while threatening to not come back. While some of this was occurring, he was trying to get Sally to go out with him. She declined his invitation, which would have been the same as asking her to hit herself on the head with a hammer. Soon, he did walk out on his new lady, after telling her what a loser she was.

Why is this a success story? Because the woman who ended up suffering could have been Sally. Instead, Sally had used the DRS: Scale Two, along with other skills she had learned and avoided another painful situation. She was proud of herself for avoiding this fate. Sally had learned how important it is to take time and find healthy men who are free of DRS.

## Instructions for Scale Two

If you are in a relationship or interested in another person, you will need to do this scale twice: Once to evaluate yourself and again, to evaluate the other person. Where the questions have a blank space, you will need to fill it in with the name of the person whom you are evaluating.

For example, Is . . . . generally a likable person? If you are doing Scale Two on yourself, you would mentally put your name in this space. When you are evaluating another person, mentally put their name into the empty space.

Each question is to be answered based on a five-point scale. The score can be from zero to five with five being the highest possible score for a question. The highest possible score for the complete test is 100 points. Only someone who can walk on water or part the Red Sea will score this high. For the rest of us, a score of 81 or more is excellent.

When someone scores between 61 and 80, which is very good, the prognosis is also very good. If the score is between 41 and 60, it suggests things are average. There are probably some areas to be concerned about when the score is in this range. The closer the score is to 60 the better are the prospects for a successful relationship.

A score, which falls between 21 and 40, suggests the presence of significant problems. These problems will probably need to be dealt with if a relationship is to have any chance of being successful. Even then, it will take time, commitment and effort to shape the situation into a healthy one. I do not mean to imply that this range of scores suggests an impossible situation. It does mean that if you do not work on the areas suggested, the prognosis will be poor.

Also, the person whose score falls within this range, may need to seek professional help. Where you or the other person scores within this range of 21 to 40, I would strongly suggest caution about entering into a new relationship. If you are already in a relationship, this kind of a score will help you know what areas need improvement. Professional guidance may make it easier to resolve these issues.

Where an individual scores at 20 or below, it suggests the person probably needs professional help. At this level, it is likely the issues are too complex to be resolved with any self-help approach. You can also expect that any relationship, where either scores this low, will be filled with pain and disappointment. Also, it will often be very volatile.

## DRS: Scale Two

Five Points = Excellent
Four Points = Very Good
Three Points = Average
Two Points = Below Average
One Point = Needs Work
Zero = Very Poor

1. Is . . . . a generally likable person?
   Is. . . liked by your friends, his or her friends and your family?

2. Does . . . . treat people kindly and with consideration?
   This includes service personnel, such as sales clerks, waitresses and waiters and, Is. . . considerate of those he/she does not particularly like.
3. Does . . . . express ideas and positions clearly?
   Are these ideas and positions well thought out and reasoned before being presented?
4. Is . . . . respected by friends, co-workers and peers?
   If your family or friends know him/her, do they respect him/her? (This is different from liking the person).
5. Is . . . . dependable?
   Does . . . . keep his or her word? This includes both personal and business matters. Can you rely on her/him?
6. Is . . . . flexible?
   Open to new ideas and information from others; Willing to try new things, places, food, people, music, etc.
7. Is . . . . tolerant of others and the differences in people?
   This is nearly the exact opposite of being too critical in speech and attitude.
8. Does . . . . run his/her life ethically and fairly?
   Has a basic code of ethics and conduct with which he/she responds to people and situations? (Also known as having character).
9. Does . . . . devote time and energy toward improving him/herself and growing as a person?
   This includes taking classes, reading, learning new skills, attending seminars, etc.
10. Is . . . . self-confident and self-reliant?
    Has a realistic belief in his/her abilities and skills, Runs his/her life effectively.
11. Stays on Course?
    Does not get sidetracked by unimportant side issues; Does not take on so much that she/he cannot finish; Does not get bogged down in detail.
12. Does . . . . objectively consider facts and options before making decisions?
    Avoids making impulsive decisions; Thinks before making important commitments.

13. Does . . . . Accept disagreement with his or her positions with grace and good nature?
    While willing to be assertive about what he/she believes, recognizes other people have a right to their views and opinions.
14. Does . . . . show determination to obtain desired results and goals?
    Does not get discouraged easily; Has a history of finishing what is started.
15. Does . . . . Communicate with honesty?
    A willingness to say what needs to be said rather than saying what others want to hear; When asked for an opinion, he/she tells the truth.
16. Is . . . . not unduly swayed by opinions and positions of others nor their anticipated responses:
    Again, willing to accept disagreement but will only be swayed or change positions due to objective factual reasons.
17. Does . . . . handle stressful situations and events with a reasonable degree of calmness?
    Does not become hysterical or overwhelmed by normal, everyday stressful events? (I am not referring to things like seeing a murder or a friend dying, or events of that caliber. Rather, I am referring to not getting a raise, someone saying bad things about you, getting a traffic ticket, etc.).
18. Is . . . . effective at negotiating solutions when a problem arises?
    Willing to attempt compromise with others to get desirable results and to resolve situations; Avoids cutting own throat in order to win.
19. Does . . . . avoid acting impulsively?
    Able to defer instant gratification and to plan for medium and long term results; Avoids making snap decisions or conclusions, unless the situation demands immediate action.

20. Does . . . . treat him/herself with respect?
Takes good care of him/herself physically and emotionally; Moderate habits without engaging in any really bad or dangerous habits; Does not put him/herself into dangerous situations, nor engage in unnecessary, risky life styles.

## DRS Scale Two: Keeping Score

After you have answered the questions, either for yourself or for you and another person, you will need to do some thinking about the results. Of course, the total score will be informative. This score may help point you into a more useful direction. At least, the score can help you to know you and your Significant Other in a more productive way.

Next, you need to look specifically at questions where the score was two, one or zero. If you had any scores like this, you now know what areas you will want to improve. By listing those areas, you are forming a map, which will point you in a better direction. Further, by knowing where you scored low, you also know what you need to change.

Let us say you scored yourself a two on question five: Is . . . . dependable? You can decide you will practice being more dependable. Perhaps, you will make a special effort to be on time, if this is an area you have some difficulty with. Maybe you will only allow yourself to commit to things you know you can finish. Whatever your difficulty with being dependable is, you can change it.

Anyway, as you list those questions where you did score low, you will be giving yourself a gift. One of my instructors said, "the first step to any change is to become aware of the problem. Without awareness, you cannot know what needs to be changed." Your awareness is really the gift of knowing what you can change. By making those changes, you will become a better person. You also improve your chances for having a successful, happy, relationship.

If you are considering someone as a Significant Other, your evaluation of this person will be of incalculable benefit to you.

You can know, before you jump in, what lies ahead. What if the total score for this person is very low? You may want to consider making a choice to avoid a relationship until there have been some changes. Unless you love restoration projects and pain is fine with you, this is the choice I would suggest.

What if the total score is acceptable but there are areas where the score was low. You will need to make a decision. If the person you are considering is flexible (question 6) then he may be willing to hear what you have to say. Also, this person may then be willing to improve that particular area. What if this person is not willing to listen or work on those areas where he scored poorly? Do you think it bodes well for your future with this person?

Often, a person who scores high average (near 60) or better, is open to working on himself. Here, an honest talk about what you have discovered and what you would like to be different, may do the trick. You must also be willing to talk about what improvements you need to make. I would recommend you ask the other person what changes they would like you to make. Fair is fair unless of course, you are already perfect.

How another person handles this kind of honesty can tell you a lot about him. If he is closed off and unwilling to listen, do you really think he will see the light if you wait long enough? What if he turns the whole thing into a contest of whose fault all of this really is? Does this tell you something you need to consider? Of course it does.

What if he responds in helpful ways? Let us say he considers what you have to say and is honest with you. This would help you to know he is willing to put out some effort to make a relationship work. I know this would make him a much better prospect for a future relationship then the man who wants to place blame.

## Already Committed

If you are in a relationship, what you learn from DRS: Scale Two may be good news or bad news to you. Where your relationship is basically a good one with some problem areas, what you have learned can really help you. You will see what behavior you need to improve for yourself and your relationship. By making personal changes, the relationship itself will usually improve. Your improved behavior may encourage your Significant Other to also make some changes.

From DRS: Scale Two, you will also gain a good idea of just what you want your Significant Other to change. This will help you to be specific about what you want, without making it about blame or whose fault it is. With this approach, it will make it easier for the other person to acknowledge those areas she or he may need to improve.

If your relationship is in serious chaos, then what you learn may be seen as bad news. The DRS: Scale Two will force you to face just how bad the situation really is. Earlier, I said if your relationship was too far gone, this book would probably not save it. A really bad relationship is usually not worth saving.

If this is true for your situation, I am sorry. However, knowing the truth will at least make your choices much more clear for you. Also, you will have a better idea of what the real prospects are for your relationship to succeed. If the prospects are bad, I hope you choose to give yourself a better future.

## Paula and Alan – Ten Years of Misery

Paula and Alan have been married for almost ten years. Each has a history, which suggests Destructive Relationship Syndrome has controlled their lives. Their ten years of marriage have been very hectic to put it politely. They have consistently bickered, blamed each other for all the problems. Both appeared to have settled for a life of low-level misery.

When Paula first came to see me, her focus was on enlisting my help in forcing Alan to change. At first, no matter what I did to get her to work on herself, she would distort the results. By the time she got home from a session, she had turned the session into being all about Alan. She would then lecture him on all his faults and use me as the authority for this criticism.

This behavior led him to believe I was in cahoots with Paula. Together, we were out to make him the bad guy. Because of this, he refused to have anything to do with me. When I suggested they see someone else, he refused. He was convinced he would get a "raw deal" from any therapist I suggested.

Finally, things got so bad, neither of them could stand it any longer. Each went to see an attorney and they were close to divorcing. I asked Paula to think about how expensive a divorce would be. Since she was already worried about money, this piece of information really got her attention. She finally began to listen to what I had been saying. For the first time, she admitted her whole purpose in seeing me, had been to force her husband to change.

I gave her my DRS: Scale Two and asked her to do it, first herself and then on Alan. However, she was not to mention anything about it to Alan. Since he was so angry with her and me, I knew he would not listen to anything either of us had to say. Paula was told to put her attention on those areas where she scored in the lower ranges. I suggested she come up with a plan for making changes in those areas where she scored poorly.

When I saw her next, there was a significant change in her attitude. She had been shocked to see what her total score was and the number of areas where she had low scores. Although I had talked to her about many of these areas, until she did the test, she just did not hear me. Paula now admitted her marital problems were at least half her doing and maybe more. This was a breakthrough for her.

I helped her with her plan of action. Also, I got her to promise me she would stop asking Alan to change. Instead, she would spend one month working only on herself, particularly the areas where she had scored low. I asked her to tell Alan what she had learned about herself and her contributions to the problems they were having. The most difficult thing I asked her to do was to apologize to him for having blamed him for all the problems.

Three weeks later, Alan called and asked me if he could see me. When he came in, he told me he was surprised at the changes he had seen in his wife's attitude and behavior. According to him, she talked to him in a "softer more gentle way." Also, he said she was not busy pointing out his faults. Because of how different she was, he had decided I was not out to get him. He knew it was time for him to look at the part he played in the problems they had.

These two people continued to change their own patterns of Destructive Relationship Syndrome. They called the divorce off and began to enjoy being with each other. As each changed his or her patterns, it became easier to be more patient with the other person. Within a few months, the only divorce needed was for them to divorce me.

This case underlines the potential for change that is possible when you are willing to look at the truth about yourself and your Significant Other. If you are willing to do something about changing your patterns, amazing things can happen. DRS: Scale Two is a helpful tool in knowing the difference between what is really happening and what you might wish to believe or imagine is happening.

I cannot urge you too strongly to take the DRS: Scale Two. It will help you see your strengths and your weakness. Also, it will give you a much clearer idea of how the Significant Other in your life really is - not how you want to believe he or she is. With this information, you improve your chances of improving your life and your relationships.

## POINTS татакTO REMEMBER

1. DRS: Scale Two will help you to identify those traits which contribute to having a successful relationship. It will also help you to see what patterns have caused or will in the future cause problems in your relationships.
2. Your knowledge about patterns, which lead to painful relationships, can help you to avoid falling into destructive relationships.
3. If you are in a relationship, DRS: Scale Two will give you a blueprint about what needs to be improved.
4. How you or a Significant Other scores on the DRS: Scale Two, can be a predictor of how your relationship or potential relationship will fare in the future.

CHAPTER 10

# *The Second Secret*

In Chapter 1, I revealed the first important secret to being freed from Destructive Relationship Syndrome. It is, *A Good Relationship Is an Easier Way to Live*. As I pointed out, this secret will also help you to know quickly, if your current relationship is basically healthy or beset with the symptoms found in DRS. If your relationship or current S.O. is making your life more difficult, confusing, chaotic and even painful, you are probably in a DRS situation.

Together, let us imagine a very different scenario. You are not now in a relationship and you do not now have any S.O. in your life. Additionally, you have moved beyond your own DRS condition. You are, for the most part, a happy, well functioning person. Your life is working well and you have decided you are ready for a significant relationship. Do you know the most important question you must ask and answer before you move toward creating a relationship? *My bet is, you do not!*

This is not a trick question. Yet, it is a question I have rarely heard anyone ask. When I ask individuals in workshops and my private practice, what they think this question is, I get many responses. Someone will say, "Is she a good person?" Someone else will say, "Does he have a good job or career?" Another common response is, "How attracted am I to . . . ." I have heard "Does he have money?", "Is she good in bed?" "Does she attend church?" or "What is his religion?" "Is he good with children?" I am sure you can add many questions to this list.

Each of the above questions deserved to be considered and answered. However, not one of those questions is really the most important single question, which you must ask and answer for yourself. Even if you get the answers you want to the kinds of questions I have just mentioned, you still will not know what you really need to know.

## A Question and Answer

Before we proceed, I want to give you another work assignment. I want you to write out what you think the single most important question to ask, might be. If you believe any of the questions I have mentioned is the one, write it down. Feel free to write out as many questions as you wish. If my suggestions are not what you consider to be the one, you can create your own.

This assignment is not a test nor is it designed to make you see yourself as uninformed. This is a step in your education. I think, until you know the question and the answer, you are not ready for a new relationship.

What if you are already in a relationship? This question and its answer can give you a new sense of what needs to be done to improve your relationship. You will have a better sense of direction for your relationship. With this new [common] sense of direction, perhaps you can begin to shape your relationship into one that works and works well. **Please take a few minutes to do this assignment.**

## Heads or Tails – A Joke

Before I reveal the answer, I want to tell you a joke. You could easily construe this joke as sexist. However, it makes a good point about the subject under discussion. I first heard this joke from Howard Ruff, a financial newsletter writer. It is about a man, in his middle forties, who is divorced. [This joke could just as easily be about a woman].

His divorce had been painful for him, emotionally and financially. As a result, he had made himself a promise – he would not make the same mistakes again. Also, he would be much more selective about the woman he considers for his next relationship. He knew it was important to take time to get to know the other person.

After a few years have passed, he believes he is ready for a new relationship. He begins to actively date. After a time, he finds himself drawn to two particular women. He wants to choose between them, but he cannot decide which one he should choose. Each has unique qualities, which he believes are important.

Since he is attracted to both, he continues to see them both. However, he knows he wants a committed relationship – not casual dating. He knows he must make a choice but which one should he choose?

In the hope it will make it easier for him to decide between the two women, he devises a little test. He decides to test how both of them handle money. His choice for a test is based on the importance he places on money issues. Also, money issues played a role in his divorce and he does not want to go through those problems again.

Our hero gives each woman One Thousand Dollars. He tells each that the money is a gift and they are free to do what they want with it. He does not tell either that it is a test, nor does he even hint at what the consequences of the test are.

The first woman buys him a designer tie, which cost One Hundred Dollars. Also, she asks him to take her out to a gourmet dinner, which will cost about two hundred dollars. She wants the dinner to be at a fancy restaurant. This is so she can show off the designer outfit she bought with the rest of the money he had given to her.

The second woman buys him a Twenty-five Dollar bottle of wine to thank him for the gift. Also, she takes him out for a good but modestly priced dinner. At dinner, she shows him a receipt from a major mutual fund, where she has put the remaining Nine

Hundred Dollars. This mutual fund has averaged 15% growth per year over the past ten years.

Here is a question for you: Which one do you believe he will choose to be his Significant Other? WRONG! He chooses the one with the great body.

If you are honest with yourself, I am sure most of you have made just such a frivolous choice sometime in your past. I am equally sure, you lived to rue the day, as the romance writers might say it. Building a relationship on such trivia is similar to building a house on quicksand.

Not only did our hero not know the right question to ask, he did not even care about the answer. If he is lucky the woman who handled money well, also had the great body. This might help him to avoid one problem in his relationship. As for the other problems looming ahead, he has left his fate up to fate. This is a great way to end up very unhappy.

The man in this joke, has made one of the most important decisions in life based on one of the least important factors. I am not saying there is anything wrong with wanting an attractive person. I am saying attractiveness should be way down on your list of important considerations. At a minimum, surely it should not be the only consideration.

## You Must Ask the Right Question!

Here at last, is *The Question*! You must ask and answer the following question for yourself. "**Exactly how do I want my life to be?**" Until you know how you want to live your life, now and in the future, you cannot possibly know what kind of person will fit into your life. The slot machines in Las Vegas will give you better odds of being a winner.

It does not matter if you meet the *perfect* person, whatever this means to you. If his life plan is very different from yours, you will be in trouble! I am not referring to differences in taste but rather the issue of how you will live your life in general. This means basic philosophies, life style goals, types of friends, children, religion and more.

Let us say you see yourself living a low key life, in a small town and your S.O. to be, is a hard driving corporate type. I can almost guarantee you, this kind of difference will produce serious problems. And love will not overcome them. Both of you may try to avoid the consequences of this difference – for a time. In all likelihood, the issue will bubble to the surface and cause tension and disagreement.

You must be very honest with yourself about this question and your answer. If you lie to yourself, or practice denial, you are setting yourself up for pain and disappointment. There will be a steep price to pay for your practice of self delusion. You see, no matter how nice, loving, successful, or wonderful the other person is, it will not stop the relationship from blowing apart . . . if each of you has a different answer to this question.

Over the years, I have worked with couples whose lives had been miserable for each person. Yet, there was nothing really wrong with either. Rather, after a time, the real differences in what each wants out of life finally came into the open. If these differences were substantial, which is usually the case where the couple is seeking help, then anger and hurt are also on the surface. Most often, each believes he or she has been cheated by the other.

What if she wants a traditional life style, including children and staying home to raise them, while he wants to build a business and wants her to help? Will there be any dissensions? Of course there will! The only question is how soon. What if he has always dreamed of having a place by the beach, with a boat, while she has always wanted to live in a rural environment? Given the passage of time, what each wants will cause a struggle between them. Very few couples could negotiate this kind of problem with success.

Now, let me add another piece to the equation. What if he is not very comfortable with little kids and she loves children? No matter how much they love and care about each other, the relationship will probably not last. If they do stay together, one of them will end up totally unhappy. They may compromise so that both end up with an unhappy life.

While compromise for the benefit of everyone is usually a good thing, these types of compromises are not.

"The worst and best are both inclined To snap like vixens at the truth. But, O, beware the middle mind That purrs and never shows a tooth!" Elinor Wylie (1885-1928), U.S. novelist. Nonsense Rhymes. The Columbia Dictionary of Quotations is licensed from Columbia University Press. Copyright © 1993 by Columbia University Press.)

## Don and Beth – The Schism

When it came to running their lives, Don and Beth handled things well. However, when it came to their relationships, they did very poorly. Each had been in several unsatisfactory relationships. Both had picked Significant Others who had difficulty taking care of their own lives. Often, the people Don and Beth chose, had a history of relationships which had failed too.

Don had been raised within a very traditional household. He was essentially, what most people would call, an old-fashioned type of guy. Beth, while also raised in a traditional type of family, was really into her work. Although her mother had been a homemaker, Beth was dedicated to having a successful career. She was proud of the fact she was the first person in her family to graduate college.

Not only did Beth like her work, she also valued her independence. As she put it, "I do not want to end up depending on a man, like my mother had to do." When it came to children, Beth had made a decision. She did not want children in the near and possibly far future. Perhaps, after she had made it in the business world, she thought she *might* take time off to have a child. She really was not sure about this.

Don was saving his money to buy a small ranch. He lived very frugally and almost hated the Los Angeles area. He definitely did not want to live in a city any longer then was absolutely necessary. Don *quietly* believed men should make all the major decisions and women should go along with those decisions. Of course, he would always consider what his wife wanted but he would make the final decision. Don wanted a large family. In his mind, this would include at least three children.

When Don and Beth met, both were coming out of a serious relationship, which had ended badly. Each was still affected by the breakup and was going through some emotional difficulties because of it. Both were lonely and while neither would admit it, each wanted to find someone fast. In their minds, getting involved with someone would help get them past the pain.

Their first date went very well. They each felt comfortable because they got along so well. Beth found Don's gentleness to be refreshing. She had previously been involved with abusive men. They also shared a love for skiing. Of course, his idea of skiing was to go to a little out of the way place, while Beth liked the major ski resorts, such as Aspen. Neither said anything about this difference. Beth said she liked horses and wanted to own one some day. This pleased Don, because he too wanted horses on the ranch he hoped to have one day.

On subsequent dates, they continued to get along extremely well and their mutual attraction grew. If a subject came up, which might prove to be a sore point, they were quick to change the subject. Neither wanted to risk having the other upset. (This behavior is called conflict avoidance and it is not a positive sign for a relationship.)

While Don and Beth realized there were some differences between them, neither believed they were very important. What was important to each was that they got along so well. Their relationship was growing into the best either had ever had . . . and sex was good too. Also, each was pleased with the lack of any significant disagreements. It was their conflict avoidance, which gave the appearance of an absence of disagreement.

After just a few months of dating, they got married. Shortly after the marriage, they had their first crisis. Don had found a house, with some land, near the mountains. He wanted them to move there as fast as they could. Beth was dead set against moving out so far from her work. For her, it would mean a two to three hour commute each way.

Don was determined to move. He had even worked out a deal with his company, which allowed him to work from his home. After talking with Beth about her concerns, he suggested she quit her job. When she objected, he said she could find a job, which allowed her to work at home. This would mean leaving the job she loved and this she did not want to do at all.

They had many arguments over the issue of moving. This became a constant battle. Beth finally decided to give in and she agreed to move. As she said, "I did it for the sake of our marriage." However, she remained adamant about keeping her job. Not only was she successful at it, she knew that she had a great future with this company.

Underneath her agreement, she was filled with deep resentment about moving. She believed that Don was being unfair about what she needed. While she kept this little secret to herself, she was seething inside. In her mind, Don was showing an insensitive side, which she had not seen before.

Within a few months after the move, Beth was very frazzled. Her job, which was very demanding, was now taking more of her time as was her commute time. She was not getting enough sleep and her anger at Don was beginning to grow stronger. This anger made it hard for her to fall asleep at night. Beth told her doctor about this and he prescribed sleeping pills. The pills caused her to be groggy during the day.

The combination of stress, lack of sleep, the pills and her anger caused Beth to lose all interest in sexual intimacy. Don responded to Beth's loss of sex drive by putting pressure on her to become more sexually active. The result of this pressure was an increase in the level of Beth's anger. She began to avoid Don and to spend more time at her office. This led to more unhappiness for both of them.

## The Little Escape

After several intense arguments, Beth told Don she could not go on this way. She told him that buying the house had been a mistake. Beth wanted to put the house up for sale and to move back into town. Don disagreed with this and would not hear about selling the house. He loved the house and the rural area and did not want to ever live in a city again.

After many battles, Beth suggested a compromise. She would take money from her premarital savings and buy a little condo near her work. This would allow Beth to stay overnight on those occasions, where her work caused her to stay late. Also, from time to time, she would stay in town when she wanted to get together with her friends for dinner. Beth missed being with her women friends.

What Beth failed to tell Don was the whole truth about what her real goal was. Her primary reason for suggesting that they buy a condominium was to "get away" from Don, all their bickering and to have time away from her marriage. She believed that *little escapes* would help her to stay in the marriage. Beth did not anticipate what Don's next move would soon be.

While Don did not like the idea, he agreed to it. This was because he could see how tired and upset Beth was and he hoped this would solve the problems they were having. When he agreed, Beth was pleased. She also thought it would at least go a long way toward solving their problems. Also, it told her that Don did care about her and was willing to compromise for the sake of their marriage.

They stopped fighting and began to get along much better. In their spare time, they kept busy looking for a condo. Don being Don, he did not want Beth to consider anything without him being there. "Everyone knows women are not as good at business things as men are," was his position.

While Beth wanted to pick her own place, she let Don select the one she finally bought. Beth knew Don did not like or want this compromise in the first place. She thought if she let him pick the place and take care of the negotiations, he would feel better about their agreement. Beth hoped that things would now calm down. Things did calm down but only for a short time.

Within a few months, Don made his next move. He began to pressure Beth into getting pregnant. Beth responded to this pressure by finding reasons to spend more time at her condo. She also began to look for ways to go out of town on company business. Don knew what was happening and he was very unhappy with how things were going. They were soon spending lots of time arguing – again.

One night, during what seemed to be their never ending bickering, Don told Beth she had lied to him. He told her she knew he wanted children and now she was unwilling to consider getting pregnant. In Don's opinion, Beth was trying to change the rules of the game. He also pointed out he had compromised about getting the condominium, so she too should be willing to compromise. To Don, this meant Beth should be willing to get pregnant.

By now, Don and Beth were very unhappy. Each was experiencing high levels of stress too. When they were not arguing, they were not talking to each other. Beth was staying away from home frequently. They started to fight about this too. After another intense argument, they decided to seek help. This is where I came into the picture.

At our first meeting, it quickly became clear to me, neither had asked nor answered *The Most Important Question* for himself or herself. Therefore, they had not asked each other this question. They did not have a clue, as to the question much less the answer. If you can imagine driving in the fog, blindfolded and in a strange town, then you can understand what Don and Beth were doing.

While each had a vague idea how he or she wanted his or her life to be, neither had a firm idea nor even a semi-clear picture of the future. This meant they had never considered how they wanted their joint lives to be. From what they had already told me, I could see that their differences were considerable.

For their first homework assignment, I asked each to ask and answer *The Question*: "How do I want my life to be?" I told them to answer this question in as much detail as each could think of. To help them get started, I suggested they include the following: Where did s/he want to live? What kind of house did s/he want to live in?

Also, I asked them to include what kind of friends each saw himself or herself having, what kind of career s/he wanted, how many children did s/he want, and the kind of entertaining s/he wanted to do. I suggested each also write something about vacations, investment goals and anything else, which seemed important.

What I was asking them to do, was put on paper, exactly how each saw himself or herself living life in the future. I also asked them to avoid any discussion about this assignment. This included not showing the other what each had written. We agreed to discuss the answers during our next session.

## Two Photographs

By now, I am sure you have a good idea about what they would soon discover. Imagine two photographs showing two very different life styles. His photograph would show a small ranch, in the foothills, with horses and other animals all around. There is a pickup truck in the driveway and there are several children playing in the yard.

Her photograph would show an office, filled with very modern furniture. There is a sign on the door, saying Vice President [at least]. In her reserved parking space, there is a BMW or Mercedes. On her desk is a photograph of a contemporary home, in an affluent area, close to the suburbs. The lawn is immaculate and so is the pool.

During the next session, I had them read what the other had written. They were shocked to discover how different their *photograph*s of life were. As each began to develop his or her own vision of how he or she wanted to live life, it was not a complete surprise to either. Deep down inside, both had a fairly good idea of what they had wanted. Neither had ever put it into some concrete form.

What did surprise each of them was discovering how different the other's life style goals were. While Don and Beth knew about differences between them, neither thought these things were important. How could Don or Beth clearly say what he or she wanted? Neither had asked nor answered the question: "How do I want my life to be?" If you do not know what you believe, it will be difficult for you to tell anyone else. No wonder Don and Beth were surprised.

Too often, while in the heat of our passions, we avoid asking the questions we need to ask - not only of the other person but of ourselves as well. Until we have asked and answered the question about how we want our own life to be, we cannot even know what to ask of the other person. Instead, we are trying to put a puzzle together, without any idea of what the finished product should be. And, we are trying to do this, while blindfolded with at least one arm tied behind our backs.

## A Little Plea

Please take my word about this issue. If you have not asked and answered the question, "How do I want my life to be?" do so. Until you have, you are not ready to even consider finding the *right person*. Actually, without the answer to this question, you are playing emotional Russian Roulette and this is dangerous.

Oh, before I forget, Beth and Don divorced. While both tried very hard to solve the problems of their marriage, the problems won out. There were too many differences for them to bridge. No matter how hard they tried, they could not find the solutions, which both could accept.

I want you to take time and consider the question, "How do I want my life to be?" Think about it before you attempt to answer it. If you can, form a mental image of how you would like to see yourself living. In this image, put in how your home will look and where it will be located. Also, put in where you would like to work, the kind of friends you want to have and the life style you want for yourself.

Remember to include your income goals, whether you want children or not and if you do, how many? Think about the kinds of places you want to visit for travel and vacations. Also, put in your attitudes about church and religion, if you want pets or not and what kind of pets. Include anything you think of which may be important to you.

Next, write all of this information down on paper. Write out your thoughts as they come to you. Do not edit them. Also, do not try to make what you write politically correct. You are forming a special type of map for you to follow. This should encourage you to make your map as accurate as you can. (We will talk more about map making in later chapters).

After you have written until you seem to run out of words to write, stop. Take a break. Then go over what you have written and put it into some kind of order. Start with the most important aspect and move on down through the list. You may need to do this several times. It is well worth the effort, unless of course, you have learned to enjoy having destructive relationships!

By the time you have finished this assignment, you will have a very good idea of what kind of person you need to seek out. If you are not in a relationship, you may be surprised at what you have discovered about yourself and your previous relationships. If you are in a relationship, this assignment will help you to know the areas you and your Significant Other need to deal with. Perhaps, these areas are open to negotiation and the kind of compromises, which work for you both.

## Points To Remember

1. Until you have asked and answered The Most Important Question, you are playing Russian Roulette with your relationship life.
2. It is important to write out, in detail, just how you want to live your life. Include how you want to live it now and in the future and your future goals.
3. Often, we avoid asking the very questions of ourselves and others, which would help us to have good relationships and a more successful life.
4. If you are in a relationship, the answers you get from asking The Most Important Question, can help you get on a better track. You and your S.O. can then come up with a plan that works for you both.

CHAPTER 11

# *The Question of the Year*

I am about to expose you to what I not so humbly call, ***The Question of the Year***. What you learn from this, can help you to change the path you have been following throughout your life. If you take to heart what you will learn, your life will nearly always get easier and better. This will be true for you and for your relationships too. The Question of the Year will also help you develop some specific goals. These goals can make your relationship happier, healthier and much more successful.

If you are not in a relationship at this time, what you learn will be at least equally valuable. The Question of the Year can help you know if someone will be in your best interest. With what you have learned, you will quickly know if the other person suffers with Destructive Relationship Syndrome. Of equal importance to you will be having knowledge about his outlook on life. The Question of the Year will show you what outlook on life works and what kind of outlook will spell trouble for you.

I know what I have said about The Question of the Year is a lot to promise. Please do not allow the simplicity of what you discover to distract you from its power or importance. When speaking of simplicity, Walt Whitman (American Poet 1819–1892) said it well: "The art of art, the glory of expression and the sunshine of the light of letters, is simplicity." (Leaves of Grass, 1855).

By resolving to follow what you learn from The Question of the Year, you will be pleasantly surprised with your results. You can become a happier person, who gets past your problems more quickly and with less wear and tear. These good results can be obtained from knowing and putting into action the answer to The Question of the Year. While it will require that you expend effort, what you gain will make it worth this effort.

## History of the Question

Over the years, I have collected many articles, studies and general information, which compared happy, successful people with those who are neither. When I refer to success, I am not talking about money, a big name or a career. I am talking about being successful in the way a person leads his life. This encompasses his entire life style and includes family, friends, relationships, career and more.

Along with what I collected, I have also talked with hundreds of people who fit into both sides of the equation. Then, after seeing the results of a recent study, I decided to put all this information together. Once I did this, the Question of the Year just popped out at me.

What you will soon discover is not just my opinion. The conclusions you will learn about, are based on a combination of all the information I had gathered and assembled. Other organizations and people came to the conclusions I had reached. I was only the assembler of the disparate pieces of information. Of course, these conclusions support what I believe to be true for all of us.

My next step was to reduce all the possible conclusions to just five. I also reduced the findings to direct, simple and useful information. While I did create the Question of the Year, I want you to keep in mind that most of the work, information and conclusions leading to the question were the result of the work done by many people other than myself.

Lastly, after devising the Question of the Year, I tested it on many people. I asked men and women to rate the quality of their lives and then to answer the Question of the Year. In my practice, I had several dozen people answer the Question of the Year. With a few exceptions, the results were always the same. I will tell you more about those results after you have had the opportunity to read and answer the Question of the Year.

I cannot emphasize too strongly the value of what you can learn from the Question of the Year. Of course, I am assuming you will be honest with your response. If you decide to give the answer you *think* you should, you are only cheating yourself. One of your reasons for reading this book, should be that you want to stop cheating yourself.

Even if you do answer with something less than the truth, you will still learn something valuable. If you decide to ignore what you learn, I will be sorry for you. This is because I know you will experience great difficulty changing your life if you do not apply what you learn. Until you apply what you have learned, you will find that your life and your relationships will continue to be what they have always been.

I know these are harsh predictions for me to make. This is how important I believe the Question of the Year can be for you and your relationships too. By answering the Question of the Year, you will at least know more about the attitudes and outlooks of happy, successful people. Also, you will find what you learn is simple to apply.

## Question of the Year

Before you begin with the Question of the Year, there are a few things I need you to do. First, I want you to imagine it is really possible to achieve what the Question of the Year implies. I am not saying it is or is not possible. Next, I want you to imagine how your life would really be if you could accomplish what the Question of the Year suggests.

After you have read the Question of the Year, read the possible answers I have provided. Then, to the best of your ability, decide which answer comes closest to what you believe the results would be. Only after you have picked your answer will I want you to read what the answer is. Again, it is not my answer. The answer is a combination of answers taken from all the studies I collected, combined with the interviews I have conducted with people.

If You Could Eliminate all the negative influences and factors, which are in your life now, would your life be:

1. Completely free from stress and much happier and more satisfying?
2. Mostly free from stress and much happier and more satisfying?
3. Moderately free from stress and somewhat happier and more satisfying?
4. Somewhat free from stress and somewhat happier and more satisfying?
5. Little changed in either the level of stress or dissatisfaction?

Please decide which answer comes closest to what you believe would be true for you. After you make your decision, write a brief statement, giving your reasons for believing this would be your result. Again, avoid trying to give the *desirable or right* answer.

> "It is always the best policy to speak the truth, unless of course you are an exceptionally good liar." (Jerome K. Jerome (1859-1927), British author. Idler (London, Feb. 1892). The Columbia Dictionary of Quotations Copyright © 1993 by Columbia University Press.)

Keep the following in mind. I have asked you to imagine it is possible to eliminate all the negative influences in your life. To imagine this, you will need to think about what negative influences are in your life right now. You should include any people, situations or circumstances which reasonable people would call negative influences. Please stop reading and finish answering the Question of the Year.

## Answer to Question of the Year

The answer will surprise most of you. Again, I want to remind you, it is not my answer. It is the answer arrived at by many people after several studies that were done at various universities and clinics. The answer simply combined the results of these things.

The answer to the Question of the Year is number five: If you could eliminate all negative influences and factors, which are in your life now, *there would be little or no change in your level of stress or your dissatisfaction.*

The studies suggested it is the positive aspects of an individual's life, which decide the quality of a person's life. It is not the mere absence of negative factors. *Groups and individuals who felt very positive about their lives had no fewer negative influences than those who were very unhappy with the condition of their lives.*

Those individuals who tested high on balance and well-being *did not have fewer stressors in their lives compared to those who tested low in balance, well-being and satisfaction!* There was a key difference which separated this group from the group that was unhappy with their lives. It was their involvement in hobbies, social relations and interactions, physical activities and being active in other than work related activities.

One distinct pattern really separated the two groups. This was the degree of positive activities a person had in his or her life. If you found a high level of positive activities in someone's life, you could predict that the quality of their life would be high. Your prediction would prove to be correct. Conversely, if you could see the level of dissatisfaction and unhappiness a person had, you could predict accurately, how uninvolved that person was in positive activities.

One major study, which was cited in the Wellness Letter (University of California at Berkeley, Vol. 11, Issue 2), concluded: "... too much emphasis has been given to eliminating (all) negative experiences and not enough to teaching people (how) to develop positive aspects of life."

This study underscored the importance of adding positive factors into an individual's life. One of the conclusions was that adding Positive Factors into a person's life would help reduce stress and enhance the general quality of his or her life.

Many studies have suggested that illness and stress related disorders are higher in groups without sufficient positive factors in their lives. People are often too busy with *nonessentials.* They often are left with too little time to pursue the essentials.

These studies suggested that essentials included time for friends and family, taking care of one's health and having time to think and reflect. Also, it is important to make time for hobbies, learning new things and getting into nature from time to time.

# Making Nice

One significant study was conducted by Robert Levenson, Ph.D. from the University of California at Berkeley and John Gottman, Ph.D., now at the University of Washington. This study focused on married couples. Dr. Levenson and his associates were looking for what factors might be predictors for a successful marriage. Following are a few of their major findings:

Successful couples focused on the positive aspects of the marriage and each other! The researches found that successful couples averaged five positive remarks for each negative remark or criticism uttered. Each also made statements, which showed an appreciation about the good points, attitudes and attributes of their spouse. Perhaps even more significant, each considered the other's faults to be but a small part of the other's personality.

When Levenson and Gottman looked at unhappy couples, the differences were dramatic. These couples put most of their attention on problems within the relationship and life itself. The ratio of positive remarks to negative ones often fell below one to one. Instead, these couples vocalized lots of complaints about their spouses. (I have worked with couples whose ratio is at least five negative comments for every positive statement made.)

My personal experience, working with individuals and couples, supports what Doctor Levenson and Doctor Gottman have published. Unhappy people often spend most of their time focused on all the problems in their lives. These people are quick to tell you about every disappointment and upset they have. Yet, they find it difficult to talk about what is going well or what could make them happy.

Unhappy couples spend most of their time talking about what is wrong with their relationship and each other. Complaints and gripes seem to be the only thing they have on their minds. I have listened to many recordings of couples' disagreements, which lasted for fifteen minutes or longer. One couple set some kind of a record. They recorded one conversation that was nearly four-hours of mutual complaints.

There are a few things that have always struck me about many of these recorded disputes. Often, neither person has said one nice thing about the other. Also, the issues they begin to talk about often get lost in the piles of negative comments. Rarely, do either offer any solutions to what are called "the problems."

This focus on complaints and problems leaves these unhappy people with too little time for what would make them feel better. Even what they read usually has to do with problems. Also, they often surround themselves with people who are just as unhappy. Then they can spend all their time talking about what is wrong.

When I look at happy people and couples, the contrast is striking. These people devote most of their time to what enhances their lives. They enjoy life, their friends, family, jobs and hobbies. All these positive factors reduce the impact of negative incidents, which can happen to any of us. Instead of locking onto what was wrong, they stayed focused on what goes well in their lives.

Another important finding, contained within some studies was related to the idea of gratitude. Those people who tested high for balance, satisfaction and happiness, evidence a high degree of gratitude for what was good in their lives. They did not discount how hard they have worked to make their lives satisfying. Still, they had a sense of gratitude for how well their lives were going.

This sense of gratitude is nearly always missing in those who are unhappy and dissatisfied with their lives. Unhappy people often believe everything should go perfectly for them. In their view, if any one thing is wrong, then life is no longer any good. One study even suggested that unhappy, dissatisfied people often negated or denied what was going well in their lives. Instead, nearly all of their attention was directed toward what was not happening the way they hoped or believed it should.

## Sylvia – No Pleasure

Sylvia had a very responsible job, which included high pay and an impressive title. She lived with her husband and child, in a nice area by the beach. She drove an expensive car, wore designer clothes and was in excellent health. Yet, she was sad, filled with stress and fed up with the grind her life had become.

I asked her to make a pleasure list for me. This list was to include the hobbies and activities she liked or might like, if she were to try them. Also, she was to estimate the cost of each, from free, to moderate or expensive. Lastly, I asked her to write down how long it had been since she had done each activity.

When she came in for her next session, she had finished her assignment. As she handed the list to me she said, "No wonder I am so unhappy. When you see my list, you will know what I mean."

Her list surprised me. I did not think she would have thought of many things she believed were fun or interesting to do. I was wrong. Her list contained twenty-five things she liked to do or would like to try. These included, riding a bike, hiking, walks on the beach, dancing, making love (remember, she was married), horseback riding, taking off to find out of the way places to stay and a lot more.

Most activities on her list were either free or were priced moderately. The problem was in how long it had been since she had done anything on her list. She had not been hiking in five years, nor had she been dancing in many years. It had been almost one year since she had gone bike-riding. While she liked making love, it had been many months since her husband and she had found the time.

Sylvia understood what all this meant. If you do not do any of the things, which bring you happiness, growth, pleasure and knowledge, how can you expect to be happy? Her whole life was dedicated to work and solving everything that in her mind was or could become a problem. All positive aspects had been *surgically* excised from her life. She did not even do things with her child, which I would call fun.

When Sylvia had first come to me, she was sure it was her marriage that made her miserable. After she had made her list, she was able to change her mind. I told her I wanted her to begin doing things from her list. Also, I wanted her to discuss her interests with her husband and get him involved. While I wanted her to do some of her list by herself, she was to also include her husband in as many of these activities as possible.

Over the next weeks, Sylvia became a much happier and positive person. She even carried herself with a bounce in her walk. Friends told her she even looked younger. Sylvia began to have fun being with her child and her marriage steadily improved. Because of the changes he saw in Sylvia, her husband became willing to change his work schedule to spend more time with her. I wish all situations were resolved so easily.

If you are in a relationship resolve to put positive aspects into your life and the life of your relationship too. Sit with your Significant Other and come up with a plan of action. This plan should be directed toward putting positive things back into your relationship. Ask questions and find out what your Significant Other likes or might like. Your S.O. will be much more flexible if your plan includes activities which interest each of you and both as a couple.

If you are not in a relationship, make your own plan of action. List ten activities you might enjoy doing. Your list should contain a mix of activities. Include anything you can think of. Call your local paper. Often, a newspaper has a specific day when it publishes lists of interesting activities, classes, lectures. Also, newspapers publish information about social activities taking place in your community.

Other good sources are City Magazines. For example, in Los Angeles, there is a magazine by that name. Most cities have some kind of publication which will tell you about interesting activities going on in that city. Do not overlook local community colleges and community parks and recreation services. These sources will give you plenty of activities to consider.

## Banking the Positives

I do not know of anyone who looks forward to receiving an unexpected and expensive bill. However, if we have extra money in the bank, it is no big deal. If we are barely making it, an unexpected bill is a very big deal. It could cause us many problems. A sudden large bill could even force us out of our homes or even worse. A savings account might just save us.

In life, some bad things will happen occasionally. If we have many positive factors in our banks, we can probably handle most things well. If our personal (positive) bank account is overdrawn, any negative bill has the potential to put us into bankruptcy (pain). I cannot urge you too strongly to begin putting more positive aspects into your life – right now.

I know most people would rather spend time with people whose lives are interesting and inspiring. You can become much more this way, if you make your life more interesting. The more positive aspects you put into your life or your relationship, the more exciting, happy and successful you and your relationship will be.

## Points To Remember

1. Putting into practice the answer to the Question of the Year, can help you become a happier person. It can also help your relationship to become more successful.

2. Successful couples use far more positive comments then negative comments about their Significant Other and their relationships than do unsuccessful couples.

3. Studies show that putting too much emphasis on eliminating what is wrong, often will contribute to the unhappiness we may experience. Instead, we need to learn how to develop the positive aspects of life.

4. Learn to have gratitude for all the positive aspects and opportunities in your life. It will help you develop better balance.

5. Create your own list of classes, lectures and pleasurable, interesting activities. Include things you have done or would like to do. Then, begin to do them.

7. If you are in a relationship, get your S.O. to help create a joint list of activities, hobbies and classes you both could do together.

## Information:

*"Information can tell us everything. It has all the answers. But they are answers to questions we have not asked, and which doubtless don't even arise."*

**Jean Aaudrillard** (b. 1929), French Semiologist. *Cool Memories*, ch.5 (1987; tr. 1990).

## Chapter 12

# *The Journey Continues*

Before we continue with our journey, I need to emphasize an important point. Breaking free from Destructive Relationship Syndrome will require a conversion of beliefs and actions in two separate areas. Each area works synergistically with the other. However, it is the first area which facilitates change within the second area.

I will go even further. If you do not make changes within the first area, you will find that making any changes in the second area will be difficult. Sometimes, it may even be close to impossible.

The first area concerns initiating changes in personal beliefs and behavior. Common sense tells us when an individual is beset with fears, insecurity and unhappiness, he or she will have a full time job just trying to survive. There simply will not be enough time, energy or desire left for anything else.

Also, as I said earlier, we often seek our own perceived level. An insecure, unhappy person usually finds a person with similar insecurities to be in a relationship with. So while both areas of change are important, personal change is perhaps more so.

The second area for change is directed toward the patterns of behavior which can improve the quality of your relationships. If you are in a relationship now, these skills can help make it a much happier and more successful one. If you are not in a relationship, this second set of skills will help you to find someone with whom a relationship has a good chance of being successful and satisfying too.

## A Question of Esteem

There is one key, which is central to nearly every pattern to be found within Destructive Relationship Syndrome. This key concerns Self-Esteem or better said, the lack of Self-Esteem. Individuals who are free of DRS have found some way, which allowed them to develop sufficient self-respect, security and Self-Esteem. As a result, these individuals usually find themselves in happy, successful relationships.

I have worked with some individuals who, while lacking some Self-Esteem, were still free of DRS. However, I have never found a person beset by DRS who did not have low Self-Esteem. Individuals who suffer from low Self-Esteem usually manage to get themselves into chaotic and unhappy relationships. A bad relationship reinforces their sense of low Self-Esteem.

In my office, I sometimes hand a dictionary to a person I am working with. I ask her to look up the word *Esteem*. When she has found the word, I ask her to read aloud a few of the key parts of the definition. Here is what Random House Webster's College Dictionary has to say:

"To regard highly or favorably; regard with respect or admiration; . . . Favorable opinion or judgement."

Next, I ask her to add the prefix, *Self* to the above definition. We usually arrive at the following definition we can agree upon: "To hold oneself in high regard and to have respect for oneself. To view oneself in a favorable light and to judge oneself as having high value."

Then I ask the following questions: "What does any of those definitions have to do with what someone else thinks about us? Do you see anything in the definitions, which has to do with impressing others, getting their approval or their agreement?"

No matter the answer I receive, I will then ask her to look up the word, "Pander." Here in part, is what the dictionary says: "A person who caters to or profits from the weakness or vices of others." Now I ask, is someone who panders to get love, approval or even acceptance, working on Self-Esteem?

In reality, someone who panders to get love or approval is simply lowering their Self-Esteem. The lower it gets, the more willing to pander she becomes. Very soon, she will have very little and perhaps no Self-Esteem left. This will cause her to sell herself short and lose more Self-Esteem.

Self-Esteem is not something anyone else can give you. You will not find it in a box of Cracker Jacks. I wish I could give you some secret formula or a magic wand, which would create Self-Esteem for you. To the best of my knowledge, neither exists. Instead, I will bluntly say, we must all get Self-Esteem the old–fashioned way. We have to work for it and earn it.

"Self-Esteem (is) Success over Pretensions." William James (1842-1910), U.S. psychologist, philosopher. The Principles of Psychology, vol. 1, ch. 10 (1890).

Throughout this book, I present processes and approaches, which will help you to earn Self-Esteem. I attempt to make it as easy as possible but it will still require you to make some effort. It is not always easy to change the beliefs, attitudes and behavior, which have contributed to maintaining low Self-Esteem. Often, it is hard work.

I hope you will not fall into the pattern alluded to by Paul Watzlawick, in his book, "The Language of Change" (Basic Books, Inc. New York, 1978). Here is what Dr. Watzlawick has to say: "There is no such thing as piano playing. I know because I tried it once and nothing good came of it."

Those individuals who have earned sufficient Self-Esteem, usually expect most things will work out well. They are usually right. Even if things do not work out as they would like, these individuals have a sense they will handle the problems. Also, they know they will be OK. Those individuals with low Self-Esteem, usually expect the worst to happen to them. They also doubt their abilities to survive the catastrophes, which they are sure will soon befall them.

For individuals with low Self-Esteem, the results are these: The more they have, the more fearful they become. The more fearful they become, the more often they make bad decisions. These bad decisions lead to the very (bad) things they fear. Because of this cycle, individuals with low Self-Esteem usually end up in a constant state of anxiety. As we have already discussed in Chapter 8, anxiety often contributes to Destructive Relationship Syndrome.

When we look at successful, healthy, happy couples and individuals, we will find the exact opposite from the attitudes found in those suffering from DRS. While these individuals are not blind to problems, they are optimistic about the outcomes. They put most of their focus on what is going well. One powerful result of this positive outlook is that their interactions with their Significant Others are usually productive and positive in tone, affect and effect.

## A Car of Your Dreams

During a session I often ask someone to imagine she is going to be given a gift of two million dollars. However, this gift comes with one condition: The recipient must purchase an automobile costing between eighty thousand dollars and three hundred thousand dollars. I ask the individual to decide just what car would fit this dream.

Because people are different, I have heard the car described as a Rolls Royce convertible, a Mercedes or a Porche and others. What car they choose does not matter, provided it is very expensive and preferably, one they would like to own. Next, I ask the person to specify the color she would like. Then we agree to call this her *Dream Car*.

Now I ask, "Would you park your dream car in a gang or slum neighborhood? Would you lend your dream car to a known drunk or an individual who has a history of many auto accidents? Would you leave your dream car unattended for long periods? Would you haul loose fertilizer in this car? How about piling junk on its finish?"

The answers I have received from every person I have posed these questions to, is always an emphatic, "No!" When I explore why the individual would not do any of these things, the answer I get always comes down to one idea. The car is too valuable to do those things to it.

At this point I say, "So you would treat a machine with more respect and care than you treat yourself. Is it because you see the car as having value? What does that say about how you value yourself?"

Unfortunately, people with lousy Self-Esteem do believe they are less important then almost everything else. Instead of learning how to change their poor self-evaluation, most individuals with poor Self-Esteem try to feel better by causing something outside themselves to change. Until they have at least as much respect for themselves as for a *dream car*, they will continue to suffer as will their relationships.

## Seeking Levels

Many psychologists agree that we all tend to seek our own *perceived* levels. The operative word here is perceived. When an individual *sees* himself as a loser or someone without much worth, he will often create a life fitting his perceived level. His relationships will reflect his perception. The bad news is, he is the problem. The good news is, he is also the solution.

As an individual begins to change his opinion of himself, he will begin to feel better. This leads him to act with more confidence. He will also begin to attract healthier people to him. This of course will lead him to finding a healthier woman with whom to enter into a relationship.

After all, the higher the value he places on himself, the better he will treat himself. He also will expect and even demand better treatment from others. This leads him to avoid those who treat him badly. Simultaneously, he will begin to find those people who will treat him with respect. These two things will help him to improve his Self-Esteem.

What if he is already in a relationship? His increased Self-Esteem will lead him to respond in more constructive ways than in the past. This often leads his relationship into a more positive phase. Where a relationship is worth saving, this alone may be the catalyst, which leads to a good, happy and workable relationship.

I cannot emphasize enough, the power of change that is possible when just one person in a relationship begins a journey toward Self-Esteem. His journey will produce effects on all the people around him. To be with him will require that they find different ways to respond to him. Those people who value him, will make the effort to respond to him in new ways. What of the ones who do not value him? He does not need them in his life.

As we continue, I will offer you many techniques and processes, which can help you to move onto the path of better Self-Esteem. Most are fairly simple and straight forward. Do not let their simplicity fool you. We learned our low Self-Esteem through simple processes too. Yet the results of these processes, often haunt people their entire lives.

For example, I tell a child repeatedly, he cannot do anything right. This would teach him, in a very simple way, to believe he was inept. What if I added to what I said, the implication he will not be accepted or loved because he cannot do anything right? Will his fear of rejection be far behind? Of course not. Yet, these *simple methods* can and often will leave a mark for many years.

One study concluded that over 85% of all the communications between adults and children could be classified as negative. We have learned to emphasize to children what we do not like or do not want instead of what is positive and constructive. I have had parents tell me they were not supposed to comment on what their child is doing right. One father said, "He is supposed to know what is right. Why should I have to compliment him for that?"

Simple phrases, such as, "Bad boy (or girl)!", "What's wrong with you – Can't you do anything right?", "Get away from me. I can't stand being around you." and "Why can't you read (or . . .) as well as Bob?" often produce painful results. The effects are even worse if these things are said in a harsh tone of voice. They undermine a child's sense of confidence, competence and Self-Esteem. Put bluntly, the parent's emphasis on the negatives helps tear down a child's Self-Esteem.

Too often, children who have been talked to in these ways, grow up to be adults who do the same thing. These adults then talk to other adults in a similar fashion. This will include their Significant Others and their children too. And the beat goes on.

# Finding Dog Poo

In an earlier chapter, I wrote about Self-Fulfilling Prophecies. The term has become a cliché but like many clichés, it is one because it is based on something real. The types of Self-Fulfilling Prophecy we are concerned with are those which predict bad outcomes. People with low Self-Esteem usually expect just that – bad outcomes.

Anyway, along with poor Self-Esteem, come lowered expectations. Lowered expectations often influence the person to create exactly what he fears. This fits the accepted definition of a Self-Fulfilling Prophecy. If we expect the worst, we often make it happen. This leads us to conclude that the lousy opinions we have of ourselves must be valid. This leads us to even lower Self-Esteem.

A professor was attempting to impress on his students, just how a Self-Fulfilling Prophecy could come about. To demonstrate, he asked his class to participate in a project which would last for one month. This project would show how Self-Fulfilling Prophecies influence the results we get.

First, the students were to write the following: My goal for the month of (?) is to find quarters every day. Additionally, each night before going to bed, they were to close their eyes and picture themselves finding quarters somewhere in their usual environment. Each morning, they were to say aloud, "Today, I will find quarters." Again, they were to close their eyes and visualize themselves doing just that.

The results, were as you might expect. These college students found money – not just quarters but money in many denominations. One young woman found a one hundred dollar bill.

The professor was not yet done. Tongue in check, he asked them to decide if they could find the money because, a) They had developed the psychic ability to communicate with money; b) They could create money out of the elements; c) They had developed telekinesis and moved the money by the power of their minds; d) They found the money that was already there. But, until they expected to find money, they had overlooked it.

Of course the answer is obvious. Yet, I do not think the professor went far enough. After they had reported their results, I would have liked him to have divided the class into two teams. He could have called them teams A and B.

I would have him take Team A aside and tell them the following: That on a specific street (we will call it Main Street), people were growing lots of flowers. He would then tell them they were to go to Main Street and estimate how many different flower gardens there were. Also, they were to estimate how many different kinds of flowers are growing in these flower gardens.

After Team A left, he would then tell Team B that on the same street, people were not careful with their animals. As a result, there was a great deal of Dog Poo on that street. Their task was to estimate just how many piles of Poo there were on Main Street.

When Team A returns, they will report on all the flowers they have seen. What will Team B have found? The Dog Poo! Yet, both teams walked the same street. It just depends on what each team expected to find. It is the expectations, which leads you to find just what you expect. This is what Self-Fulfilling Prophecy is all about.

The lower an individual's opinion of herself is, the more she expects to *find the Poo*. With her low expectations as her guide, she will go and make herself right. She will find the Poo! Put another way, she will be successful at what she would be better off failing at. Until she changes her low Self-Esteem, chances are nothing will change.

I want you to make a decision. Starting now, you will practice looking for the flowers. You will stop looking for the Poo. While I am not asking you to ever ignore the Poo, I am suggesting you spend more time looking for what is going right in your life. The next techniques you will learn will help you find more of the flowers and less of the Poo.

## Three for One

Earlier, I discussed how those who suffer from DRS are often very negative in their patterns of thought and speech. In this chapter you have read how lousy Self-Esteem goes with poor expectations. Poor Self-Esteem and poor expectations lead to a negative outlook about almost all aspects of life. Then, as you have learned, this combination produces self-fulfilling prophecies, which will control much of our lives.

Individuals who have developed a negative mind set are often unaware of how negative they are. They often find negativity objectionable in others. Yet, they will continue to find the fertilizer in every garden, while overlooking all the flowers. Sometimes, these unhappy people will deny the existence of flowers – at least for them.

Where each person in a relationship, suffers from Destructive Relationship Syndrome, the negativity is overwhelming for all concerned. I have heard couples who appear to be in a contest to see who can be the most negative. Each works at topping the bad comments of the other. Neither of them seems to understand what the prize for winning this contest is.

Anyway, if an honest look at yourself reveals you do tend to be negative, I offer you what I call Three for One. Three for One requires you to use three positive statements for every negative one you think or speak. This positive ratio will slowly but surely help you to retrain yourself.

To make Three for One effective, you must make a commitment. You will need to pay attention to your thoughts and to what you are saying. Each time you hear yourself saying something negative, you must immediately follow up with three positive comments. These positive comments need not be anything of great import. They could be such as, "Gee, it was really a beautiful day and I had a good workout at the gym. I am really looking forward to reading a good book tonight."

If, instead of verbalizing a negative statement, you find yourself thinking a negative thought, the same rule applies. You need to immediately think of three events, things or aspects, which are positive. For example, you find yourself thinking, "No one ever listens to me!" You would then say to yourself, "I am proud of myself because I got a lot done today. I really enjoyed our dinner last night and I am looking forward to going dancing this weekend."

As I have said, the purpose of Three for One is very direct. It is to retrain yourself into being more focused on the positive aspects of life, which are all around you. Please do not expect your transformation to be an instant one. If you have discovered you are negative in your outlook, it is a good bet you probably have been practicing this for many years. You are good at it. Give your self some time and your mind set will change. Do not fall into the trap of the man who tried piano playing once and nothing came of it.

Of course, you could take a short cut. Decide to be a positive person. Then you can avoid doing this process. I can accept this. You will find, if you become more positive, it usually improves all aspects of your life. Of course, you can expect it to improve your relationships too.

I do want to warn you of what could be a temporary problem. If you are someone who fits the definition of a negative person, some people may be confused as you become a more positive one. Do not conclude it is because they do not want you to be a happier person. They are simply used to you being and acting in certain ways. Give them a little time and they will adjust. Most of your friends and loved ones will like the change in your attitude.

While I suggest patience with any and all changes, you do need to find a middle ground. Please do not put off practicing being more positive because you have plenty of time. Nor do you want to invent excuses, which will allow you to continue your painful path. The sooner you produce a change, the sooner you will begin to reap the rewards. As Hector Berlioz said, "Time is a great teacher. Unfortunately it kills all of its students."

As your practice begins to take effect, you will notice a change in the way you think and express yourself. Along with these changes, you should also begin to sense a more optimistic attitude in general. This will lead you into feeling better about yourself. In short, you will have added to your Self-Esteem by your efforts. Your effort helped you to restructure your thinking. To the old philosophic homily, "I think; therefore I am," we can add "and as I think, so goes my life."

It is not an exaggeration when I say changing how you think can and will help you change your life. It will also change your relationships. Shifting how you think is very important. In the next chapter, I will suggest a few additional methods to help you to do just this – change your thinking.

## A Little Inventory

Think of seven to ten people whom you know. I want you to mentally divide them into two specific groups. In one group, I want you to place those whom you would honestly categorize as essentially positive people. In the second group, put those whose main tendency is to be negative. Then, for the next week or two, pay close attention to how all these individuals express themselves.

Here is what I am sure you will find. Those whom you consider positive, will usually talk in a positive way. They will also have a generally optimistic attitude about life. Conversely, those in the negative group will often use many negative phrases. Usually, they express a negative attitude as to their lives in general. Now notice which group seems to have their lives going well and which group seems to live in a state of tension and stress.

Lastly, decide which group you want to belong to. I am sure that you will want to belong to the group whose lives seem to go more smoothly. So it makes sense to copy what they know and do. Your Three for One assignment will help you to develop one important set of skills found in positive people.

## Relationship Strategy

I would also like to suggest a new method for dealing with your Significant Other. Decide to find at least three things to compliment your S.O. about *each day*. If you have discovered you are someone who fits the label *a negative person*, it is a pretty safe bet, you have shared your negativity with your Significant Other. Please believe me when I say, if you have been negative to your S.O., she or he has some anger, hurt and sadness because of this.

By saying at least three positive things a day to your Significant Other, you will begin to change the tenor of your relationship for the better. You may even find your S.O. begins to be more complimentary to you. At the minimum, your new behavior will put a stop to any cycles of negativity which have taken over your relationship. Try it right now. I know you will like the results.

Also, when there is a problem to be addressed, find a way to include Three for One. If your S.O. has a habit of being late and is late meeting you at a restaurant, try this. "I know how hard you work. You are generally very thoughtful. This is a great restaurant you selected. I am disappointed you were late. I would like it if you could be on time. At least, call to let me know you will be late."

The above example combines Three for One and a method I call Four Steps Communication. You will learn more about this in Chapter 15. Anyway, by focusing on the positive aspects of your S.O., he will have less need to argue or be defensive. This will make him feel more comfortable. Instead of feeling attacked, he will recognize the positive tone of your message. Also, this will make it easier for him to be willing to work on finding a solution.

Three for One can make a valuable change in your relationships. Again, be patient with yourself. It will take some time to get comfortable with using more positive statements. You will find it well worth the effort and your Significant Other will be pleased, after he gets past his surprise.

## Points To Remember

1. There are two distinct areas to be focused on. The first is personal change. The second is about changes which affect relationships.
2. Self-Esteem: To hold yourself in high regard, treat yourself with respect and care. No one is handing out Self-Esteem. You obtain Self-Esteem by working for it.
3. You must treat yourself with at least the same regard you would show to something you value – your car, home, pets, etc.
4. We all seek others who match our perceived level. By learning to see ourselves as having value, we will seek others who also see themselves as having worth.
5. Poor Self-Esteem is often linked with negative Self-Fulfilling Prophecies. We then expect the worse and make it happen. This only adds to poor Self-Esteem.
7. Eighty-five percent of communication with children is considered negative. We must retrain ourselves to have a positive outlook.
8. Three for One. Learn to say three positive things for each negative you speak. Also, use the same ratio for negative thoughts.
9. If you are in a relationship, give your Significant Other at least three compliments each day. When discussing problems, find some way to also mention good points about your Significant Other.

## Chapter 13

# *Golden Rule Days*

School Days, School Days – Wonderful Golden Rule Days. I wonder how many of you remember this little ditty? Robert Fulgum, in his wonderful book, "All I Really Need to Know I Learned in Kindergarten" said it well. He believes that most of what we really need to know, we learned in grade school a long time ago. While I do not entirely agree we learned all we need to know, we did learn plenty.

When we were children, our teachers relied on many tools trying to educate us. Two of these tools will always stand out in my mind. They are, the ubiquitous blackboard and flash cards. Well, blackboards are now sometimes green. A few are even pink. To me, whatever their color, they are all blackboards. Anyway, so much of what we did learn as youngsters included the use of blackboards and flash cards.

Because blackboards and flash cards played such an important role in how we learned, I want to take you back to those old Golden Rule days. I developed two techniques, which are based on the use of blackboards and flash cards. They will help you to change your negative thoughts, beliefs and behaviors.

One of these will have you using an imaginary blackboard. The other will have you using flash cards. However, both are different from those you used in school. These techniques will help you to develop a more positive attitude about yourself and your life. This will lead to a better self-image and to developing higher self-esteem.

As you may recall, I said that breaking free from Destructive Relationship Syndrome requires two sets of skills. One set of skills is directed toward changing the way you see yourself. The other set helps mainly with relationship issues. This Chapter is about the first set of skills. The skills I will tell you about, will help you to make personal changes.

When we feel good about who we are, it makes it easier for us to make good decisions. This helps us to conduct ourselves in healthier ways. Both results are conducive to finding and maintaining relationships which are successful. While this chapter is about how to help change you, it also will make a positive difference in your relationships.

My Blackboard and Flash Card Techniques are easy to learn and to use. They produce powerful results. I may sound like a broken record but I need to say something again. It will take you some time, effort and practice, to get the results you want. My magic wand is still at the repair shop. So far, no one can get it working. Until that happens, I am afraid you will need to do some work.

The Blackboard Technique will help you to change negative beliefs you have about yourself. What do I mean by negative beliefs? If a person thinks he is stupid or cannot do anything right, these would fit my description of negative beliefs. No one can love me, or I am not good enough, or I can't learn are examples of negative beliefs. I am sure you can think of many more. Shortly, I will ask you to do just that – think of specific examples, which affect you.

In Chapter 3, I wrote about Self-Fulfilling Prophecy and the part it plays in DRS. I said that the combination of Self-Fulfilling Prophecy and negative beliefs, was always dangerous. This combination will lead you to unhappy relationships and a painful life. When you change negative beliefs to more positive beliefs, the results can be profound. By changing your beliefs, you will usually change Self-Fulfilling Prophecies too.

My Flash Card technique will help you to develop a new mental map. This map includes seeing yourself acting in productive, successful ways. Within a few weeks, these new images often become automatic. You will often find you are behaving like your new images. One woman said to me: "I wanted to look around and see who was responding in such a calm way. Then, I realized it was me! It happened so fast, I didn't even know what I had done."

## To Affirm or Not

Before you jump to conclusions, I want to tell you something important. You need to know that neither technique is another form of *affirmations*. I am not a fan of affirmations. From what I have seen over the years, affirmations work best for those who need them least! They seldom work well for those who most need them.

My first objection to affirmations concerns the often absurd nature of the statements themselves. "The Universe Loves Me." is a common affirmation. Well, it does not love me or you! The universe cannot love. It is an inanimate object, without emotions. A person who tells herself this lie, will find herself feeling very bad. She will feel bad quickly or it may take a little time but she will feel bad.

Why is it only a matter of time before she will feel bad? Because something will happen, which says to her, she is not loved or liked by someone. Since the Universe is supposed to love her, she must not deserve to be liked or loved. This is why the rule was broken and the Universe turned on her.

Another absurd affirmation is: "I can have it all." I want you to think about this. How can anyone have it all? Does this mean I can magically fly, win the lottery and everyone will respect me? Is all the money in the world mine? Will I live forever? Can I have every dream come true?

No one can have it all. If you attempt to believe this dribble, you set yourself up for a painful fall. The first time you find something you cannot have, you will feel like a failure. Whether you like it or not, some things will go wrong in your life. Even powerful, rich and famous people have things go wrong in their lives. And, the I.R.S is standing by to take part of your wealth too. Try telling them you can have and keep it all!

Let me examine two more affirmations. They are, "I am perfect the way I am" (sure I am) and "I do everything right." These things will be true, right after I create my own private universe and then, write my own set of universal rules. Even then, I might make a mistake or two. As for perfection, even the finest diamonds have flaws, if you look for them.

Also, if I am perfect, is there any need for me to learn new things? How about making any changes at all? Since I am perfect, why bother? I do not even need to bathe. I am perfect. (Are you a little queasy? I know I am). Would you care to be around me, if I do not bathe? Probably not – even if I claim to be perfect.

Affirmations just do not work very well. This is true even if the affirmations are given subliminally. If a man believes he is stupid and he tells himself "I am smart." what will happen? A little voice in his head will quickly say, "Bull – you know you are dumb!"

I am sure, there were many people who have told him he was smart. He did not believe them. Why should he? He does not believe himself when he says he is smart. If merely telling someone he is smart, wonderful and worthwhile was enough, hardly anyone would have low self-esteem. We know this is just not the way it is.

## A Little Affirmation Test

Here is a little test to help you understand how limited affirmations are. Think of something you would like to believe about yourself but you know it is not true. Pick something simple. For example, if you are a poor public speaker, pretend you are a great one. Close your eyes and say aloud, "I am a great public speaker." I bet it feels wrong.

Try another one. Let us say you are a mediocre tennis player. Close your eyes and say: "I am an excellent tennis player. I almost always win." What happens when you do this? Here is what happened to me while I was writing this. I began to grin because I am a very mediocre tennis player. As I said, "I am an excellent tennis player," it felt very funny. I began to laugh. There is no way I am going to believe this.

Now, select something you know is true. It could be I have nice handwriting, or a nice smile, or I am a good speller. Do not forget things like I am a good friend, or I am a good listener. When you have picked something, close your eyes. Then, say it aloud.

As you say it aloud, notice how it seems to fit. Your inner voice may be matter of fact – calm and assured. Anyway, what you believe is true, will sound and feel very different from what you do not believe is true. Go ahead – compare the two experiences.

Until we change our negative beliefs, we will not accept positive affirmations. We must have a belief, which will support the positive affirmation. Then, we will accept such statements. With a negative belief, we will only accept statements, which support it. This explains why affirmations work best with those who need them the least.

The weird thing is this: We accepted negative beliefs because of methods which are similar to using a blackboard and flash cards. As I show you how the Blackboard and Flash Card Techniques are done, you will understand what I mean.

For now, consider this. We have built-in systems, which help us to learn. These systems work just as effectively, no matter what material we are learning. We can learn to think scary things as easily as good things – sad things as happy things. Our systems do not care about the truth or the quality of what we are learning. You could have just as easily learned two plus two is seven as you did learn the answer is four.

## The Blackboard

Before you can begin using this method, there are two preliminary steps you need to take. The first step is to list the belief or beliefs you are targeting for change. To do this, you must think about the negative statements you make about yourself. These could be statements like: "I am stupid." or "I can't do anything right." or "I am not a nice person." It could be, "No one likes me." or "I am not really loveable." Trust your ability to figure out your negative beliefs.

The next step is important. You are to develop what I call counter-beliefs. A counter-belief is the belief you want in place of your negative belief. You need to avoid all or nothing statements and those that are grandiose and impossible. For example, your Targeted Belief is, "I can't do anything right." You would not want a counter-belief like, "I do everything right." It is not true and your mind will not accept it. You could say, "I do most things well. Sometimes I don't." This sounds realistic and is believable.

If your Targeted Belief is, "I am not a nice person." you need a reasonable replacement. "I am a wonderful person" or "I am always nice" are not reasonable beliefs. "I am a very nice person most of the time. Sometimes I am not," is believable. For "I am stupid," you could say, "When it comes to most things I am smart enough. With some things I am not." An easier one might be, "I am smart most of the time."

If your Targeted Belief is, "No one could ever love me," you will need to be a little creative. How about, "I haven't met everyone in the world – so I can't know that." Another choice could be, "Many people have acted loving to me. I just haven't found the right one." You might use something like, "I can learn to be more loveable." You have many choices about what your counter-belief could be.

Anyway, you must avoid all absolute, impossible statements. They will simply lead you to failure and frustration. You want your statements to be possible, reasonable, and to match reality. Sometimes, you need to come up with a few alternate counter-beliefs. Then, try each on for size. Usually, you will get a sense and feeling for the one which seems most acceptable to you.

There is another step I will tell you about. This step helps the Blackboard Technique to be even more effective. It is to use a relaxation method before you begin the Blackboard Technique. Which method you use, is not important. If you know how to meditate or use self-hypnosis, great. Both work very well. You might want to listen to classical music. The Cannon in D Major, by Pachelbel, is often used by people who meditate.

Some people find they relax by closing their eyes while doing slow, deep breathing, for several minutes. One method is to breathe in slowly, through your nose and hold your breath for five seconds. Then, you slowly exhale through your mouth. You repeat this several times, while you let your mind go clear.

Whatever works for you, go for it. I do not want you to get uptight attempting to relax. A few years ago, I saw a cartoon that made this point. It was a cartoon showing a man, who had himself tied to a bed. He was screaming at himself, "Relax – damn it, just relax." This is not a good way for you to reach a state of relaxation. Remember, KIS (Keep it Simple).

After you have achieved a relaxed state, you are ready to begin the Blackboard Technique. With your eyes closed, imagine a blackboard. Put this blackboard straight ahead in your mind's eye. (Some people are more comfortable doing this with their eyes open. This is an acceptable way to do it.) Do not be concerned if your image is hazy, dim or blurred. These things do not have much impact on the results you will get.

Now, imagine the belief you have targeted for change is being written on the blackboard. I am going to use the following as an example: "I don't do anything right." The moment you see or imagine the phrase on the blackboard, erase it. Next, you are to imagine your counter-belief is being written on the blackboard. In my example, this would be: "I do most things very well. Sometimes I don't."

As soon as you see or imagine the counter-belief, imagine you are turning to your right. Imagine another blackboard, with the belief targeted for change written on it. Let your mind erase this belief as quickly as it can. Now, write the counter-belief in its place. This is an exact repetition of what you had just done – except on a new *blackboard*.

You are to continue the same process, always turning to your right, in your imagination. This is repeated until any of the following three things occurs: The first possibility is the belief targeted for change, no longer appears when you turn to your right. In its place, you see the counter-belief. This same thing happens when you again turn to your right.

A second possibility is this: The belief you have targeted for change appears but is it is very faded. You have trouble seeing it.

While you are trying to see it, your counter-belief appears. It may even jump out at you. When you turn to your right, this happens again.

The last possibility is that the belief targeted for change appears but then disappears. This is similar to what is called a fade out in a movie. This is where the movie screen goes gray for a moment. Then, a new scene begins to appear. As your old belief disappears into a fade out, your counter-belief begins to appear automatically. You are not consciously making this happen. When you turn to the right in your mind, the same things happen again.

When any one or a combination of the three results continues to occur, after three or four turns to your right, you have finished with this Targeted Belief. Usually, this is all you will need to do with this one belief you have targeted to change. Sometimes, you may need to repeat the entire process a week to ten days later. You will seldom need to repeat the process more than two more times. Also, do not do the Blackboard Technique with more than two beliefs in a week's time.

## Flash Cards

You will find this technique to be very useful. It is simple and powerful. With Flash Cards, you are programming yourself to act in more positive and useful ways. The Blackboard Technique helps change negative beliefs. My Flash Card Technique will help you to change your behavior.

The first step you take is to define what new behavior you want. You need to keep it simple and direct. For example, you have a history of acting sad. You might want to replace sad behavior with being more cheerful. If you are tense and anxious, your goal might be to become a calmer person. Think of what you do not like. Then, decide what the opposite of this behavior would be.

Now, you need to use a simple little code. If your goal is to be more cheerful, the code would be BMC. This stands for Be More Cheerful. You might use CAR for Calm and Relaxed. For any new behavior you wish to practice, give it this type of code.

PA–MR could stand for Positive Attitude and More Relaxed. Always keep your codes to less than five letters.

Let's say you now have listed your desired behaviors and have given them code names. Your next step is to make four to six flash cards, about three by five in size. Then, pick one desired behavior along with its code. Place this code on all the flash cards. You should print them instead of writing them. Also, use large print.

You are ready to place your flash cards where you will see them often. I suggest you place one in your car. It should be where you can see it after you get into your car. One flash card should go on the mirror you use most often. You could put one in the kitchen and another should go to where you work. Do your best to find good places for all the flash cards.

The next step takes a little effort. You need to develop images of you acting the way your flash cards suggest. If you want to be more cheerful, create an image of you acting just this way. Perhaps, you could create several: One at work, one with your friends and another of you acting cheerful with your family. It does not matter if these images do not seem real to you. Once upon a time, to you, the alphabet looked strange and foreign.

## Stage One

The Flash Card Technique is divided into three stages. In the first stage, each time you see a flash card, imagine your new behavior. Simultaneously, you need to repeat what the goal is. For example, your goal is BMC (Be More Cheerful). When you see a flash card, immediately *see yourself* being more cheerful. While you are looking at this image, say to yourself, "Be More Cheerful." Continue to watch the image for three to five seconds.

Of course, since you have four to six flash cards in places you see often, you will repeat this process often every day. Let me reassure you. It will take you only a few minutes each day. Also, this stage only continues for seven to ten days. Within a few days, most people begin to notice some change in their behavior. Your flash card images begin to appear more automatically too.

## Stage Two

The next stage shortens the process. After the first week to ten days has passed, you are ready for this second stage. Now, whenever you notice a flash card, you repeat the goal to yourself. With our example, you would say, "Be More Cheerful." You do not need to consciously form the matching images.

By now, your mind has probably made the new image automatic. When you think "Be More Cheerful," the new image is triggered without much effort on your part. You continue this stage for two weeks. It is most important to continue saying the goal to yourself each time you see a flash card. After two weeks, you are ready for stage three.

## Stage Three

With stage three, all you do is leave the flash cards where you have had them all along. You do not need to do anything more. The flash cards will have become an unconscious reminder for you. Each time you happen to see a flash card, it sets into motion, *seeing and thinking* the new goal. By now, you usually notice you have become more like what you set as your goal.

After two or three weeks, you can put this set of flash cards away. Usually, you will have automated the flash card message. Now, you are ready to begin again but with a new set of flash cards. If, by now you are perfect, you will not have additional goals. If you are still merely mortal, you will still have areas of behavior to improve. Just follow the entire flash card program for any new behavior you want to instill within yourself.

I want you to exercise good judgment. Do not make your goals into grandiose schemes. Also, your goals must be about your behavior. If you make your goals about winning the lottery or about everyone loving you, the results will continue to be more of what you already have. You have no power to control lottery results. Also, you do not have power over what others do or feel.

I recommend you do not work on more than two goals at one time. If you are working on more than one goal, you can put the codes for both on the same flash card. You must make sure the combined codes are five or fewer letters. Remember, flash cards usually were simple and about one thing at a time.

## Adding it up

With the Blackboard and Flash Card Techniques, you can reshape the way you see yourself. Also, you can create new ways of behaving, which will get you better results. As the Blackboard Technique helps change your negative beliefs, you will feel better about yourself. This shift can spill over into every aspect of your life. Not only will you find your life begins to move more smoothly, your relationships can improve too.

With the Flash Card Technique, you will begin to find yourself changing how you act. A brilliant man, Andrew Salter, held that all behavior was the result of what he called "Conditioned Reflexes." His research suggested the more we practiced any behavior, mentally or in reality, the more likely we would be to repeat it. We would repeat it just as we rehearsed it.

By mentally practicing positive, constructive behavior, you are developing a new set of conditioned reflexes. You will soon find yourself acting in ways which help you to succeed in more areas of your life. This includes having happier relationships too. These results make the effort a small price for you to pay.

## Points To Remember

1. The first order of business is to make personal changes. If you continue to do and think what you always have, you will continue to get what you already have.
2. By changing negative beliefs and ineffectual behavior, you also improve any relationship.
3. Affirmations work best for those who need them the least. This is because they already have the beliefs, which will support positive ideas.
4. Not one reputable study has supported the claims made by people who sell subliminal tapes.
5. Use the Blackboard Technique to help yourself change self-defeating negative beliefs. It will also help you replace these beliefs with realistic positive beliefs.
6. Flash Cards help you to mentally rehearse new behavior. Andrew Salter (Psychologist) found that mental rehearsal affected behavior. We often begin to act as we have imagined.

## Chapter 14

# *Talk – Talk – Talk*

In Greek Mythology, there is the story of a man named Sisyphus whom Zeus sentences, to push a heavy rock to the top of a large hill. When he reaches the top, the rock always rolls back to the bottom of the hill. He must begin again – forever. This story is the Greek version of being sentenced to an eternity in Hell.

Too many couples have succeeded in creating a modern version of this Greek Tragedy. Their attempts to resolve problems by talking about them, produces the same results as does the man in this myth. Couples, whose relationships are in the most trouble, are usually always talking about what is wrong. This approach will often confuse things. It can make the problems worse or at least to appear worse then they really are.

Successful couples are too busy with living to make a career out of talking about problems. They are not looking to place blame nor to focus on everything, which is perceived to be wrong about the relationship. When there is a problem, they respond very differently from DRS couples. Their approach is to quickly find what will solve the problem and then, move on.

Also, they look for solutions which are acceptable to both. Neither wants to win at the expense of the other. This alone, distinguishes them from nearly all less successful couples. Successful couples seem to know that both must win if the relationship is to win. At the least, neither should be forced to lose.

In Chapter 13, I gave you two methods for helping you to make personal changes. With this chapter and the next, I will focus on approaches which can help your relationships to work better. These methods can also help you reduce the friction in your relationship. In this chapter, I will introduce you to four styles of communication which always make negative impacts on relationships. You will discover why these methods are so detrimental to any relationship.

In the next chapter, I will introduce you to my Four Steps Communication Method. Learning this can help you avoid the fate of the man in the Greek fable. I want you to know, nothing works always. My Four Steps Communication Method works often enough to help you become more effective with your communication skills. This method can help you in all aspects of your life.

## Bad Talking

Virginia Satir was an influential person in the field of therapy. Even after her death, her influence remains. In her books and lectures, she had much to say about the subject of communication and faulty communication styles. After she had worked with thousands of couples and individuals, she categorized several communication styles.

Most of the communication styles she saw in her work were ineffectual at best. Often, these styles exacerbated the pain each person was experiencing. These styles of communication helped to make any relationship a more painful and unhappy one. She pioneered many concepts which help people improve their relationships by changing their communication.

I want to take you through a few of these painful styles. These styles are often found in people with a history of Destructive Relationship Syndrome. If you fit into any of the following styles, you can be sure your relationships will often be in trouble. What is worse, these styles of communication almost guarantee you will seldom resolve the problems or issues, which interfere with having a successful relationship.

## The Blamer

The first style I will tell you about is what Virginia Satir called, the Blamer. This name really describes this style of communication. A Blamer does just what the name suggests. He blames everyone and everything for anything which may go wrong. What a Blamer never wants to do is accept any responsibility for what may go wrong. Even when he goofs, he will quickly find a way to make his mistake into someone else's fault.

Often, Blamers use harsh tones of voice and make sweeping accusations. When they are really upset, they will yell at nearly anyone. Of course, some kind of magic prevents them from attacking those who could respond in powerful ways. This would include a boss, or a judge or anyone who could cause the Blamer a real problem.

When a Blamer is precluded from blaming someone, he holds on to his anger. Often, he will look for any reason to find fault with someone else. When he feels it is safe, he will attack someone he believes he can attack with impunity. This can include his wife or children. It may include people he supervises.

Sometimes, a Blamer will even wag or point his finger at the target of his blame. Often, when he is standing, his body posture looks very threatening. While pointing a finger, the Blamer may lean into his target, jaw jutting out, upper body bent forward and one foot in front of the other. His voice will be loud and hint at controlled rage. Sometimes it is more than a hint.

"You are always late." "You can't ever be trusted." "If only you would change, everything would be fine." "Everyone knows it's all your fault." "Even your friends don't believe you." "Why can't you stand up to your boss?" "I am sick of your screw-ups. You can't even do the simplest things. You are a real loser." These are examples of blaming. If these statements look bad in print, imagine what it would be like if you were on the receiving end of a Blamer's tirade.

Try holding the Blamer's position for about thirty seconds. This will give you an idea what the Blamer feels like inside. To make it even more uncomfortable, add in an image of someone you are angry with. Then, imagine you are accusing this person of being at fault for everything while you are yelling. Within a short time, you will probably become uncomfortable.

With insecure people, the Blamer's approach will trigger fear and resentment. An insecure person will respond in one of two ways. With the first, she may feel compelled to defend herself against the charges the Blamer hurls at her. She launches into her defense and whatever the problem might be, it is totally lost. This often leads the Blamer to become more enraged. This is because he interprets her defense as an attack on him.

The second way an insecure person may respond is to meekly accept the Blamer's attack. When she uses this response, she may look down at the floor and say nothing. She may try to calm the Blamer down by agreeing with him. Her agreement simply convinces the Blamer he is right. This sets the stage for the next episode of blaming.

As I have said, people who suffer with Destructive Relationship Syndrome, often seek out others who live within the DRS metaphor. Imagine what will happen if both are Blamers. What will happen when they attempt to resolve any kind of problem or disagreement? Lots of arguments! Often, both yell or take turns yelling. Neither listens nor attempts to understand what the other is saying. There is almost no chance they will resolve anything.

Even where one person capitulates and allows the other to win, nothing changes. The loser is filled with resentment. She looks for a chance to get even. Eventually, she may explode from all the abuse she has swallowed. What communication style will she use then? She will usually become a Blamer and attack him.

He may accept her attack and try to calm her down. This sets the stage for his next bout of blaming her. Often, he may just increase his level of blaming her, while she is blaming him. Then we have two people, enraged and out of control. The war ebbs and flows but never ends.

In extreme situations, two Blamers can fall into violent behavior. This violence may be verbal. Too often, it becomes physical violence also. In extreme cases, a Blamer can explode and hurt someone very badly. While not all Blamers are violent, all abusive, violent people are Blamers. Whatever form blaming takes, it makes things worse for everyone.

## The Placater

Virginia Satir considered Placating to be another unhealthy communication style. I cannot agree with her too strongly. The American Heritage Dictionary of the English Language, Third Edition (Houghton Mifflin Company – 1992) defines placate this way: pla·cate – To allay the anger of, especially by making concessions; appease. Synonym – pacify.

A Placater does all of those things. She accepts all fault as hers and tries to make everything right. At least she pretends to accept all the fault for every problem. This prevents her from telling the truth, standing up for her rights or finding real solutions to problems.

With a Placater, even if a problem appears solved, it usually is not. The Placater has gone along only to placate – not from conviction the solution will work. This will be true even when the Placater is dealing with a healthy person. Instead of finding a solution, the Placater has one purpose – to placate.

Placaters feel very weak and often assume the role of a victim. When placating, a person will look down, have collapsed body posture and look defeated. Imagine someone on one knee, looking up with arms outstretched like she was begging. Now imagine a sad pleading voice saying: "It is my fault. I am sorry. Please don't be angry with me. You'll see, I will try to do better. Just tell me what you want me to do."

You might mimic the Placater position, just as I have described it. While on one knee, imagine yourself begging, with a voice that is pleading. Hear yourself taking all the blame. Keep looking up, with your head tilted back. Hold this position until it begins to feel really bad. Then, hold it for another thirty seconds. This will help you to know just what a Placater experiences inside.

As you might have guessed, Placaters and Blamers often find each other. Their relationships are filled with blaming and placating. Each communicates in ways which cannot address real issues. Picture a Blamer who is pointing his finger and screaming at the Placater. Now, imagine the Placater on her knees. She looks sad and says, "You are right. It is my fault. I will do better next time. Tell me what you want me to do."

The Blamer does just that: tells her exactly what to do and how to do it. Inside, the Placater feels almost sick with fear and buried anger. Because of her fear, she placates some more. The Blamer then blames some more. This continues until one or both are emotionally exhausted. It is usually the Blamer who finally ends this painful interchange.

I do not know about you but to me, this does not add up to a loving, happy image. Placating did not work for Nevil Chamberlain at Munich, before World War II. It will not work in relationships either. Usually, when someone placates, every situation gets worse. Also, the Blamer assumes that the Placater accepts being blamed. This encourages the Blamer to continue with his pattern of blaming.

## The Distracter

The next style I will discuss is the Distracter. As the name Distracter suggests, this type of communication is very distracting to most people. You cannot ever resolve anything when someone is into the role of Distracter. The Distracter always jumps from one idea to another and from one subject to another. You can never be sure what has been decided or even understood when dealing with a Distracter.

I want you to imagine asking someone why they went to Hawaii on a vacation. Your question asks for a simple response. The other person might say: "I really like Hawaii. We went last year and it was great, so we decided to go back." You would never get this kind of response from someone who has slipped into the roll of the Distracter.

To the question, "Why did you choose Hawaii for your vacation?" The Distracter might respond this way: "I haven't been on a vacation in a long time. Times are tough. You make more money than we do. I'll get us some coffee. It took me a long time to save up for the trip. Did you see the movie on T.V. last night? It was made in Hawaii. It really brought back fond memories."

The Distracter acts as if anything she says will be used against her in a court of law. She has learned to deflect anything, which to her, has some threat to it. You may never know what she feels threatened about. It will not matter.

The Distracter lives in a state of fear. Anything can set her off. She will then distract. "Why did you spend so much on dinner last night?" "Why are you picking on me? I picked up your shirts like you wanted. Besides, Johnny had a problem in school today. Why don't you ever help him with his homework? I will get you some more coffee."

I find it difficult to describe how a Distracter's body position is. The way she holds herself, very much matches the way she talks. A Distracter often has different parts of her body going in different directions simultaneously. Imagine her legs crossed tightly, while her upper body is leaning to the right.

Now, imagine her head is tilted left, while her eyes dart all over the place. If standing, she may point in one direction while looking in another direction. Simultaneously, her body seems to be ready to go in a third direction. Her words and sentences do the same thing – point in several directions at the same time.

The more you attempt to pin the Distracter to a specific answer, the more chaotic her responses will become. It takes the wisdom of Solomon and the patience of Job to wade through the distractions to find what the point or answer is. Most of us give up before we get to the place where we understand what the point is. We just nod politely and stop listening.

# The Computer

The Computer is someone who never met a fact, no matter how small, which was not important. This person wants to cover every contingency possible, with precise logic and in detail.

Usually, the recipient of all these bits of information is overwhelmed by the sheer volume of information. This often leads the recipient to a state of mental overload.

As with the Distracter, the listener may stop listening to what is being said. This drives the Computer up a wall. He will then find a thousand new facts to express. The Computer seems to believe that with enough detail and facts, he can get everyone to understand and agree with him. According to the Computer, if you seem to not be listening, it must be because he has not given you enough facts and details, .

In some ways, the Computer is similar to the Distracter. While the Computer sounds very logical, he still avoids getting to the point. Also, he usually avoids saying what he thinks, feels or what his real opinions are. Instead, he uses a barrage of facts and words so he will not have to take a stand. Often, the Computer lives in fear of anyone finding out who he really is. This leads him to hide behind other people's facts and opinions.

You might ask the Computer the following: "What kind of car do you want to buy?" The Computer might respond this way: "One could safely rely on a car rated highly by Consumer Reports. Studies now show that many cars have improved and one will be hard pressed to find significant differences between any of the popular models. Some people say foreign cars are better then domestic but others disagree. You must work out the price, trade in value, resale and cost per mile before you reach a logical choice."

To me, there are two interesting aspects to the above Computer's response. The Computer never answered the question and never even hinted at his preferences. And, heaven help you if the Computer happened to have all the facts about cars handy. You would soon hear more than you ever wanted to hear about all the details concerning all the cars he was considering. Of course, he still would attempt to avoid telling you the ones he was considering.

> . . . we need the curt, the condensed, the pointed, the readily diffused – in place of the verbose, the detailed,

the voluminous, the inaccessible. (Edgar Allan Poe (1809-45), U.S. poet, critic, short-story writer. repr. in The Centenary Poe, ed. by Montagu Slater, 1949).

In an intimate relationship, we are often asked to tell our significant other what we are feeling. I want you to think about asking the Computer to tell you what he is feeling. Would you really want to hear his response? Even if you want to hear it, there is a good chance you will not hear anything about what he feels, thinks or believes. Instead, you will most likely get what you have already got – more minutiae.

The Computer often sits or stands in a way I would describe as rigid – like a board. When sitting, his legs may be tightly crossed and his arms would be too. His voice will be tight, controlled and he will not smile easily. When standing, he is standing at attention. Even if his arms are crossed across his chest, he is still very stiff.

If you can, imagine someone who acts like he just swallowed something that is disagreeable to him. Another image could be of a man who is afraid he will be shot if he says the wrong thing. At the least, he seems like someone who must solve a very complicated problem. Trying to listen to him is often similar to a strenuous workout but for your brain, not your body.

While the Computer always talks like a computer, it gets far worse when he feels threatened. Then, not only will he increase his output of facts and details, he will also move further from the point. If you try to pin him down, he will become more fearful. It is not unusual for the Computer to turn into the Blamer if he believes he is being cornered. This also happens if he believes he is being made to look foolish.

Here is a question for you. Which style of communicator would you guess a Computer seems to be drawn to? You have probably guessed correctly. The Computer and the Distracter have some kind of radar, which is synchronized one to the other. This allows them to find each other as if by magic. If the consequences were not so serious, it would be funny to listen to these two attempt to resolve any problems at all. Usually, they have such a different sense of what has been said, they seem to be from different planets.

## Less Talk

No matter how much a person may want to improve her life and her relationships, she will not succeed if she uses any of the styles I have described. Things will be even more painful if her Significant Other is also stuck in one of Satir's communication styles.

In nearly every DRS relationship, the styles you have read about are the styles which prevail. Each person may talk effectively in other situations. When it comes to problems or their relationships, people who are suffering with DRS, usually revert to one or more of Satir's communication styles. This guarantees that things can only become more difficult for everyone.

## Straight Talk

While you are in the process of learning new ways to communicate, talk less and listen more. Nearly every therapist who works with couples has heard the same refrain: "We don't communicate." This is just not true, no matter how much each person believes it to be true. The truth is that most couples in crisis communicate too much. They say too much of what makes things worse and not enough of what will help.

A scalpel in the hands of a competent surgeon can do wonders. The same scalpel wielded by an amateur will often cause extensive damage. To me, the way we talk to each other often fits the description of a scalpel wielded by an amateur. Couples often do a good job of cutting each other up and causing damage. Until you learn to use communication skillfully, less is better as the saying goes.

At the start of the next chapter, I will ask you an important question about communication. The answer will not come until the end of the chapter. Right now, I want you to remember one definition of "Just a Little Insanity." It is: To continue doing the same thing while insisting on a new outcome. Couples within the grip of a DRS crisis often continue to talk to each other in ways which have never worked. Their solution is to do more of the same only do it better this time. This is "Just A Little Insanity."

## POINTS TO REMEMBER

1. Virginia Satir defined four communication styles which contribute to unhappy, failed relationships. They are: The Blamer, The Placater, The Distracter and The Computer. If you use any of these styles, you need to make a change – NOW.

2. Often, people revert to one of these styles under stress, particularly when dealing with their significant other. When this happens, each person runs the risk of inflicting more damage on the other and on the relationship.

3. While you are learning more effective ways of communicating, talk less. In the place of talking, practice listening. If your S.O. is using any of the Satir styles, you need to back off. You will accomplish nothing if you continue to do what is not working. Often, things will just get worse. (Remember the Greek Myth at the start of this chapter?)

CHAPTER 15

# *More Talk*

Soon, I will introduce you to my Four Steps Communication method. I want to ask you a question before I do. As I promised in Chapter 14, I will give you the answer to this question near the end of this chapter. Here is the question: "What are the two most important skills you need to communicate more effectively?" These two skills often change the entire tenor and thrust of a relationship.

Those individuals who can communicate in ways which often influence others, usually rely on these two skills. Every person I have met, who can motivate others, is an expert in the use of these two skills. These skills can help you to be more successful in all aspects of your life.

## A Second Question

I have a second question for you and I will give you the answer to this question soon. First, I want to give you some history about this question. When I was giving training seminars to therapists, I always asked them this question. In all the seminars I gave, no one answered this question correctly. The question is: **What is the most important purpose of communication?**

Many people have given me good answers. However, their answers were incorrect. Some answers I heard are: To be understood, To express your position, To increase intimacy, To be heard, To express your feelings and more. You can no doubt think of several additional answers. While each answer may be important to good communication, each is only a part of the main reason we communicate.

Many of you may want to object to the answer I will give to you. This is fine with me. I would only ask you to think about what I am suggesting. If you do think about it, I believe you will see how accurate my answer is. Here is my answer: **The most important reason to communicate is, to enable you to obtain the *desired* results.** What the desired might be will depend on the circumstances and situations.

If I want to resolve a problem with someone and we reach an acceptable solution, my communication has been successful. The results were those I was after. Let us say your goal is to be understood about a specific subject. When the other person acts in a way which suggests she really understood you, great. You have had a successful result. If she says she understood but continues to act in ways which suggest otherwise, you have not succeeded.

You want your significant other to know you are pleased with something he did. To this end, you send him a beautiful card. He calls and tells you how pleased he is you noticed what he had done. This is a strong suggestion that your communication has been successful. You obtained the results you wanted.

On the other hand, what if several days later he says: "It really bothers me you never thanked me for what I did." Now, assuming he received your card, he did not get the message. Your communication did not work. Here, you did not get the results you wanted.

It is where we do not succeed in obtaining the desired result that we can begin to act "Just a Little Insane." We may fall into the trap of, "I know what I mean – you must too!" When we do fall into this trap, we continue to do exactly what we have done. We do this, even though it is not working. Then, we get angry and do more of what is not working.

In my practice, part of my job is to make sure I am getting through to the other person. My personal record is seventeen different ways of trying to get the result I wanted. Then, I gave up. I gave up because I decided it was no longer worth the effort.

This does not mean the other person could not be reached. It means I ran out of energy and ideas. My communication did not work. I failed to get the desired results we needed to continue our work. This was a comment on my limitations not on his ability to understand.

If I were to delve into the many ways available to communicate, I would need to write another book. I have held three day seminars for this purpose alone. This book is not the place for a complete course on how you can improve your communication. However, as promised, you are about to be introduced to one powerful method. If along with this method, you keep in mind that you must always go after the desired results, you will be more successful.

## Four Steps Communication

I developed this method to help people to have guide lines for better communication. This method is very effective for problem resolution. It can also help you to learn new ways of approaching problems. You will find it helps you to get better results. Also, the Four Steps Communication Method will help you to stop using any of the Satir methods, which I have described earlier.

## Step One

With Step One, you will make a ***direct, simple*** statement about how you feel in response to a specific subject. Too often, people use too many words to say what they feel. Their feelings become lost in all the verbiage. One politician said, "To be successful . . . one must be able to go on in great length while saying nothing of substance." This may be fine for a politician but it is poison to a relationship.

By keeping your first statement simple, it is more likely that the other person will hear what you are saying. This increases the probability that he or she will know what it is you are going to talk about. You will also avoid being like the politician I just referred to.

Here are a few examples to consider: "John, I am upset." or "I am really sad about." or "I need to tell you how angry I am." or "When you . . . I really get scared." or "I am very disappointed that you . . ." or "Bob, I am excited about . . . ." This last example shows you this method can be used with pleasant events and experiences too.

I need to preach a little sermon to you. Feelings are neither thoughts nor opinions. "I feel happy" is describing a feeling. "The president makes mistakes" is an opinion. If I say, "I feel he is making mistakes," it is still an opinion. There is no feeling called, "he is making a mistake."

Just because I label an opinion or thought as a feeling, does not make it so. This is what I call a pseudo-feeling. Many therapists are guilty of teaching people to use pseudo-feelings. Pseudo-feelings often cloud issues and make resolution difficult at best. If I state an opinion and call it a feeling, I put you in a bad position. No matter how you respond, I can say, "Hey, that's just how I feel."

Feelings include happy, sad, excited, anxious, angry, fearful, joyous, uncomfortable and more. If you can say "I think" or "I believe" and have the sentence make sense, you are not talking about a feeling. "I am really angry" or "I am really thinking angry." Notice the last did not make very good sense. If I said I was thinking angry thoughts, I would be describing thoughts and not my feelings.

If I say "I feel that taxes are too high" is this a feeling? When I change this to "I think taxes are too high" it makes sense. This is a statement of what I think and not what I feel. I could say, "I think taxes are too high and I am angry about this." Then, I have told you what I think and how I feel. End of my little Sermon.

Before you speak about what you feel, there are two sub-steps you need to take. First, you must know what you are feeling. Then, you must decide if your feeling is appropriate to what has happened. Until you have finished these sub-steps, you are not ready to go on.

How often have you tried to tell someone what you were feeling, only to find out you did not know? What about when you have been so overwhelmed by what you were feeling, what you said made very little sense. Because of this, the other person would not listen.

If you cannot identify what you are feeling, you are not ready for the conversation. After all, if you do not know what you are feeling, how can you expect someone else to know for you? If you do expect someone else to know for you, then you are asking him to play the role of the Therapist. I have already talked about how destructive this role usually is.

Sometimes, you may not know exactly what you are feeling. When this happens, you may need to rely on a generic feeling. As an example, this could be, "I am feeling upset" or "I am feeling uncomfortable." Usually, generic feelings will be adequate to meet the needs of many situations. Again, you are not ready to discuss a problem until you know what you are feeling or at least, what the generic feeling is.

Your next task is to decide if what you are feeling fits what has happened. Ask yourself this question: "Is what I am feeling rational under the situation as I understand it?" You might ask, "Is what I am feeling appropriate to what really happened." If the answer to either is no, you must stop. Again, you are not ready to go on, when what you feel is not appropriate to the situation.

If what you feel does not fit the situation, or is not appropriate, you need to get yourself into a more useful and healthy state of mind. Perhaps you will need to ask the other person for a little time to think. You may need to tell the other person you need to talk but want to do it later. When you act on feelings, which are out of proportion to what has happened, you will sound irrational and out of control.

If you attempt to talk about a problem while you are out of control, you will lose. Even if you have all the facts on your side, you will still lose. What is more important, your relationship will lose too. This is because, if you are irrational, your emotions will bury your facts. No one wants to listen to someone who is being irrational.

Imagine John was supposed to call you Friday night but he did not. You are *furious*. This is not usually a rational response to a failed call. You are out of control and need to calm down. Until you do, you are not ready to talk to John or anyone for that matter. When you are this emotional, there is a good chance no one will want to hear you. They may be too polite to tell you this but it is usually the truth.

If instead, you are annoyed or a little angry with John, you are having a response befitting the crime. If you are not sure about your response, ask yourself the following question. "How would people whom I respect feel in the same kind of situation?" This is a useful way to judge your own behavior.

Here is another example. It is your birthday and you are meeting your friend for lunch. She arrives late and forgets to wish you happy birthday. You get depressed or are deeply sad. Are these responses rational or equal to the event? No! These are not the responses which fit the crime.

Now if you are a little sad or disappointed, fine. Even being annoyed would be rational. Deep sadness is felt when someone is ill or has died. In the absence of a terminal illness or the death of someone you are close to, depression is not a healthy response. I believe these are the only times true depression is a rational response to reality.

Assume you know what you are feeling and your feelings are appropriate to the situation. You are ready for the next step. With practice, you will find you know these things very quickly. You will also know how important it is to put off saying anything until you are ready.

## Step Two

After stating what you feel, you now go to the second step. You make a ***brief*** statement about the facts or your opinion about the event. Avoid the example of the politician – do not include too many details. Also, wherever possible, stick to one situation at a time.

If you like to confuse people, then ignore what I just said. Instead, bring up several situations and include all the facts and details you can. Use the style of the Computer. If you want to be understood and have clarity, KIS (Keep It Simple). Following are a few examples:

> "John, I am annoyed because you did not call me Friday evening as you promised."
>
> "Barbara, I am disappointed and a little sad you did not remember my birthday. I am also annoyed that you are late for our lunch date."

The above examples include the first two steps of the Four Steps Communication Method. I want you to notice how simple I kept each statement. Usually, there is no need to go into detail. The other person will know what you are talking about or will ask you for clarification. Either way, your communication avoids putting the other person on the spot.

If I say, "I just came back from Hawaii. I had a really great time." I am inviting communication from the other person. He has the opportunity to ask questions or make comments. Either way, the door is open. This is a good result.

I will not get the same results, if I should do the following *(bad)* detailed, boring description:

> "I just came back from Hawaii. I stayed five days in the Hawaii Village Motel. Boy, the weather was great. The average temperature was 78 degrees. Well, it did rain one day – what a bummer. We were four blocks from the beach. It wasn't too far to walk. We could walk to the beach in ten minutes. Of course, my foot was sore, so I didn't like the walk. I hurt it jogging a week before we went but I really like to jog. I know lots of people don't. Anyway, we had to walk slow because of my foot.

By the time we got to the beach, all the good spots were taken. We had to wander around until we could find one. Of course, with all the scares about skin cancer, we didn't want to stay in the sun long anyhow. We had to buy an umbrella and lug it with us. Come to think of it, why did we go to Hawaii? We did not want to stay in the sun very long. Next time, I will suggest we go somewhere else. Hey, I hear Lake Tahoe is great. It has great scenery. Blah – Blah – Blah."

The above example may help put you to sleep. It will not give you much opportunity to communicate with the other person. The speaker does not give anyone the chance to focus on what he might want to pursue. With the first simple statement about a trip to Hawaii, the other person has a chance to respond.

"My wife and I went to Hawaii last year. We really liked it. Did you have a chance to do any snorkeling?"

This leads to more areas to talk about. Talking should be a two-way street, unless we are talking to ourselves. Here is a little gem I borrowed from Microsoft, Encarta:

"The habit of common and continuous speech is a symptom of mental deficiency. It proceeds from not knowing what is going on in other people's minds." Walter Bagehot (1826-77), English economist, critic. "Hartley Coleridge" (1852; repr. in Literary Studies, vol. 1, 1878). (Columbia University Press - 1993)

***Your statement of the facts should be direct, simple and brief. Please!***

## Step Three

With Step Three, you are to suggest what you want as a resolution of the situation. I hope you choose a resolution which is reasonable and appropriate. Also, you want to be able to say what the resolution is, in a few sentences or less. Remember, the primary reason for Four Steps Communication, is to improve upon your ability to resolve conflicts and problems.

The goal of Four Steps Communication has nothing to do with being right, beating up on the other person, or affixing blame. Good communication does not sound like a trial. You are not the judge or jury. Surely, your goal should not be to be the executioner.

Let's look again, at the example of John failing to call, when he said he would. Here is how you might use the first three steps:

> "John, I was annoyed when you did not call me. You said you would call Friday. (Step One and Two). I would appreciate it if you would call when you say you will. At the least, let me know you are not sure you can call." (This is Step Three).

Notice in the above example, how simple and direct it is. John is not being attacked, nor is he being threatened with life imprisonment. While John may take this as an attack, people usually do not feel defensive when approached this way.

I want to give you another example. In this one, Jane is yelling at her husband Tom. He forgot to take care of some task and Jane is furious. Tom knows he goofed but he does not like being yelled at. He says:

> "Jane, I really do not like it when you yell at me. I do want to listen but it is hard when you yell. I know I goofed and I can see how upset you are. Please find another way to tell me how upset you are."

In the last example, you can see the three steps again. Also, Tom is acknowledging his part of the problem. However, being yelled at is unfair and does not help. Tom chooses to focus on this because, until they can talk calmly, there is very little chance anything will be resolved.

## Warning – Warning

Your attempt to resolve things can become interesting at Step Three. This is because, many people have learned to hide the real issues in fog. A Distracter will attempt to do just this. The Blamer will attempt to turn the tables on you. This may require dragging up other issues. Do not fall into the traps others set for you. Instead, you must redirect the talk back to the original issue.

In the example of Jane, she might say, "You are being too sensitive. Besides you did forget." Tom needs to restate his position – calmly: "Yes I did. However, I am upset with your yelling at me. I really need you to find another way to talk to me."

Even if you need to repeat the three steps several times, do so. Do not let yourself be dragged into another issue. This is the same as being asked to walk into a mine field. Most people who have a history of Destructive Relationship Syndrome, are experts in inviting others into their mine fields. Just because you are invited, does not mean you cannot decline.

## Step Four

In this step, you clearly say what the consequence will be if you do not come to a resolution of the issue being discussed. Often, you will not need this step. This is because most problems are resolved with the first three steps. Still, you must be prepared to offer some specific consequence, if the other person is unwilling to come to a resolution. This means you must have a consequence in mind. Also, you must be ready to stand by it.

You will only go to Step Four, if the first three have failed. For example, you have made three or four attempts to come back to the original issue. You have restated what you want as a resolution. The other person continues to change the subject or refuses to agree to a resolution. Now, you must go to Step Four:

Say John continues to make excuses for not calling when he said he would. He also tries to turn the problem into one about your personality. Here is how you might proceed:

> "John, I understand the points you are making. However, I am annoyed that you cannot call when you say you will, or at least let me know you may not call. Until you can do either one of these things, I will no longer make time available to wait for your calls."

In the example of Jane, the consequence might be two fold. First, Tom, after three or four attempts with the first three steps, might say:

> "I am even more upset because you are still yelling at me. I am going to take a short walk so we both can calm down. If we still cannot talk about this calmly, I would like us to have a neutral party present. Perhaps then, we can solve this problem."

If Jane continues to yell, it is a sure sign she is emotionally out of control. Tom will not resolve anything while Jane is in this condition. By taking a walk, he at least ends his part of this drama. He must be prepared to do what he said he would. If not, Jane will soon figure out an important fact: Tom bluffs and she does not have to listen to him.

I am not suggesting that anyone should just turn his back and walk away. This is rude and mean-spirited. It also adds more fuel to a fire which is already getting out of control. If you need to disengage, you must calmly and clearly say what you are doing.

> "We are both too upset to be able to talk about this right now. I need to take a walk so I can calm down. (Notice the emphasis is on the speaker calming down – not on the other person.) Perhaps we can sit and talk about this in an hour or so."

The other person may continue to be too emotional and may even be irrational. There is nothing you can do about another person's emotional state. You are not his therapist. The only person you can insure will act appropriately is you. This is your responsibility.

## More Four Steps

I want you to dedicate yourself to developing your ability with Four Steps Communication. This will help you sharpen your communication skills in all areas. It will also help you avoid many arguments, which are common within relationships in trouble. The more we argue, the deeper the pit of unhappiness we dig for ourselves and our relationships.

> "There are two things which cannot be attacked in front: Ignorance and narrow mindedness. They can only be shaken by the simple development of contrary qualities. They will not bear discussion." (Lord Acton, English historian, 1834–1902).

One way to become proficient with the Four Steps Communication Method is to rehearse. Select one or two people with whom you have a problem expressing yourself. Then, think about what typically happens when you try. Next, for each area where you have difficulty expressing yourself, write out two or three scripts which match what has happened in the past.

Your next step is to change your part of the script to match the Four Steps Communication Method. Also, put in how you think the other person will respond to your new approach. Be sure to include several different ways this person may respond to your new approach. Add in how you will respond to what he or she may say.

After you have completed several scripts, you are ready for some imagination practice. Visualize one person and practice in your mind using the Four Steps Communication Method with this person. Include how you think he or she will respond to you. With this exercise, you will begin to program your mind to respond in more effective ways. Also, your responses will begin to feel more comfortable within a short time.

## The Little Ones

If you are a parent, the Four Steps Method will help you greatly. Often, parents allow emotions and words to simply pour out. The little ones feel very scared and overwhelmed. This makes it difficult for them to hear what is being said. It makes it even more difficult to produce a good result.

Also, many parents I have worked with had a problem in common. They had trouble staying on their point when talking to their children. The Little Ones got confused and the parents became even angrier. This fits the phrase, A "lose-lose" situation. Everyone becomes upset, confused and resentful. These are not the qualities which improve family relationships.

By using the Four Steps Communication Method, you can stay focused on what needs to be resolved. This will help you to avoid attacking or blaming the Little Ones. Very soon, they will discover that they can no longer drag you away from the issue. Also, they will see you are consistent and you say things clearly. These skills will be outstanding examples for the Little Ones to follow.

## The Answer

I promised you I would answer the question I asked near the beginning of this chapter. The question was: What are the two most important skills needed to become a really effective

...unicator? You must listen and you must ask questions! *"If you want to be interesting, be interested"* (Unknown philosopher).

When you listen and ask questions, you let people know you are focused on them and interested too. This will always produce a climate for better understanding. Also, you can probably discover what the other person really believes and feels. Until you know these things, you do not really know how you should respond. This is like trying to follow a map that does not have lines on it. Unless you like to get lost, do not use this type of map.

Those couples, who have built successful, loving and happy relationships practice listening and asking questions. Each person does these things out of love, respect and caring. It is also common courtesy to do these things. DRS couples nearly always talk over each other. They are too busy playing the Blamer, Placater, Distracter or Computer to have time to listen to the people they are supposed to love.

You will need to choose the example you will follow. This choice will decide how your relationship will be. If you want to get lost, make sure you follow maps which do not have any lines on them. For those who want to break free from Destructive Relationship Syndrome, listen and ask questions.

## Points To Remember

1. Please keep in mind the most important goal of communication. It is to get the results you want. If you are not getting the kind of result you want, change what you are doing. Avoid falling into the trap of "Just a Little Insanity."

2. The Four Steps Communication Method can help you become more effective in solving problems. It is important to practice this method by writing scripts and mental rehearsal.

3. Learn the differences between feelings and thoughts and opinions. Do not call thoughts or opinions feelings. It confuses things and often prevents the resolution of problems.

4. If you are a parent, begin to use Four Steps Communication with your children. It will help you become more effective and it will teach them a very useful model to follow.

5. To become more influential and effective with your communication skills, learn to listen and ask questions.

## Communications:

*I know one husband and wife who, whatever the official reasons given to the court for the break up of their marriage, were really divorced because the husband believed that nobody ought to read while he was talking and the wife that nobody ought to talk while she was reading.*

**Vera Brittain** (1893-1970), British author. Quoted in Jilly Cooper and Tom Hartman, *Violets and Vinegar, "The Battle Done" (1980)*

## Chapter 16

## *Map Making 101*

Recently, I came across a word which looked interesting to me. I realized I did not have the foggiest idea of its meaning. To my surprise, when I looked it up, the word fit the subject of Map Making, which is what I want to address in this chapter. The word is Peripatetic and part of its definition is: An Itinerant; one who wanders without a plan; walking from place to place (Encarta – 1994). In my words, it means wandering without a map or a plan.

Too many people approach getting into or being in a relationship peripatetically. They do not have any plan, so they just wander from place to place. When looking for a relationship, many men and women appear willing to leave everything to chance. These men and women simply wander around, hoping *luck* and *fortune* will help them to find the way.

"Fortune's a right whore. If she give ought, she deals it in small parcels, That she may take away all at one swoop." (John Webster – 1580-1625, English dramatist – Encarta 1994).

Men and women often have no idea of what they really expect of each other or their relationships. Individuals and couples just wander, without a plan and wonder why they are lost. They may bemoan their fates while blaming others for their plights. Then, they continue to follow the same old paths (maps) to the same painful destinations and call it fate, bad luck or if they are New Age, bad Karma.

In his wonderful book, "The Language of Change," (Basic Books, 1978) Paul Watzlawick said that we do not respond to reality itself. Instead, we respond to our perceptions of reality. Our perceptions are based on our *inner maps*. These *inner maps* filter and shape how we see and understand reality. By understanding reality, I think Dr. Watzlawick meant our interpretations of reality.

Here is a quotation I used earlier but is worth repeating, I think it sums up the main tenets of what Dr. Watzlawick is saying: "Men are not troubled by things themselves, but by their thoughts about them." (Epictetus).

How our inner maps are created and shaped could be the subject for an entire book. While I have no intention of creating such a book, we do need to understand some factors which contribute to the creation of our inner maps. Briefly put, our inner maps dramatically affect our lives and this includes our relationships.

## Expectations

What we believe, based on our experiences and what we have learned, leads us to have expectations. Our beliefs, experiences and expectations contribute a great deal of what constitutes our inner maps. Expectations act as the compass we are using while we are following our inner maps.

It is our expectations which contribute to our success or failure in all endeavors. This will include our relationships. In this chapter and the next, we will explore the area of expectations in some depth.

When looking to establish a new relationship, single (unattached) people often lack any idea of what their expectations really are. If they do have some idea, they usually do not know which expectations are possible or even healthy. Seldom will a single person take the time to discover what a potential partner's expectations are.

Instead, single people often vacillate between two unhealthy positions: They make their expectations up as they go along, or rely on expectations they have never examined or questioned. Both approaches are examples of just wandering from place to place, without an itinerary. This is a great way to waste much time and get lost, too.

When we look at couples, we can add another set of ingredients. When entering a relationship, men and women often begin to act on the expectations they learned within their family structure. What if their family structures were chaotic? Then, each person may have expectations, which may not be rational or even possible to achieve in any situation.

To make things even more interesting, often, each person assumes the other knows what these expectations are. Also, each person may expect the other to comply with these expectations. Of course, neither one has bothered to tell the other what these expectations are. Remember, neither person may know what his or her expectations are. This makes it impossible to even attempt to tell the other person what is expected. Now, we are beginning to approach real terror.

## The Continuing Journey

Together, we have traveled a great distance – from the genesis and definition of Destructive Relationship Syndrome, through the patterns of DRS and to techniques for producing changes. I have attempted to show you many issues, which can determine the success or failure of a relationship. All of them have a bearing on the quality of your relationships.

What you have experienced along this journey has been an opportunity to create a new map. At the least, you have been shown how to make a more accurate map. What I mean is this: By changing your understandings and beliefs, you have been altering your internal map. This is leading you to the creation of a more accurate map. Without an accurate map, we have very little chance of arriving where we intend.

By knowing about Destructive Relationship Syndrome and its Disguises, the trap of Instant Attraction, Just a Little Insanity and the Patterns, which contribute to Destructive Relationship Syndrome, you have most of what you need to create an even better map. This is a map that will lead you to more successful outcomes.

Of course, I am assuming you have done your work: You have asked and answered the Question of the Year and completed your Self-Evaluations. Also, you have set aside time to practice the techniques offered, such as: The Blackboard Technique, Three for One, Four Steps Communication and Flash Cards.

## New Maps

It is time for the next level of Map Making: The creation of Realistic Expectations.

> "I know not anything more pleasant, or more instructive, than to compare experience with expectation, or to register from time to time the difference between idea and reality. It is by this kind of observation that we grow daily less liable to be disappointed." (Samuel Johnson (1709-84), English author, Encarta – 1994)

Those who study behavior agree, it is the failure to get what we expect that is the root of most of our unhappiness and disappointment. If you expect what the other person cannot or will not live up to, you will be disappointed. This will be true even when the other person never agreed to deliver what you expect.

As an example, let us say you expect someone to always understand you. The first time this person fails to understand you, you will be unhappy. Perhaps you will be resentful too. These are not emotional states which enhance intimate relationships. They are the kinds of emotional states which cause negative and painful consequences. This is not the way to increase the probability of a successful relationship.

If I expect you to always know what I am thinking, you will fail. Perhaps you will fail very quickly or within a short time but you will fail. When you fail, I could jump to the conclusion that you do not care enough to do what I expect. By jumping to this conclusion, I will need to find proof I am right. This will lead me to look for evidence to prove you do not really care enough - whatever enough may be to me.

When I have reasonable (sane) expectations, we both have a good chance of success. For example, if I expect you to listen when I tell you something, you can reasonably meet this expectation. Listening to another person is an achievable and appropriate behavior. By listening, I do not mean you have to agree with me. This would be an unreasonable expectation. I just mean I expect you to show common courtesy by hearing what I have to say.

What if you expect someone to always place what you want or need, above his or her wants and needs? This is an unreasonable expectation. Healthy people do not put aside those needs which are in their best interest. They will refuse and you will be resentful. Here is another opportunity to conclude that he or she does not really care about you.

An insecure person or one with DRS might appear to do what you ask. However, there will be a price to pay. Most likely, the other person will develop resentment and perhaps anger too. The other person may begin to act out his or her resentment or ask you to sacrifice your needs, to *balance* the books. Does either response seem conducive to improving your relationship?

## Low Expectations

One of the first things I do with people who are in relationship crises, is to help them to change their expectations. There is specific homework I give, which is to help both learn what their expectations really are. This will help them decide which expectations are reasonable and which are not.

When we discover what unreasonable expectations exist, I ask the person to change them. In place of the unreasonable, self-defeating expectations, I ask him to develop expectations, which we mere mortals can be capable of achieving. Usually, I can get people to agree there would be less disappointment and stress in their lives, if their expectations were realistic and reasonable.

Often, I will ask someone I am working with to consider how his situation would be different, if he had different expectations from those he lived by now. When someone has low expectations of his job or of his friends, how would his life and relationships be different if he were to raise his sights? Most people can see quickly how different things would be. Of course, he will need to have realistic and obtainable expectations.

One woman who was in an abusive relationship, had this to say: "If I believed I could support myself and that someday I would find someone who would love me, I would leave ..... in a flash." She had unrealistically low expectations of herself and her husband. These low expectations kept her trapped and unhappy.

When it came to herself, she was saying she was too inept to take care of herself. Her expectations of herself were so low as to need a magnifying glass to see anything good about herself. Also, she always had an excuse for her husband's behavior. What she was really saying is, she did not believe (expect) he could control himself.

When I met with them together, he too said he could not control himself. I told him he was expecting too little of himself but he disagreed. Then I asked him to imagine the following: He is very angry with his wife and about to strike her. Just as he is raising his hand to hit her, a big, ugly guy jumps in front of him. This guy is holding a gun pointed right at his (the husband's) old family jewels.

The man says, "If you hit her, I will blow your B . . . s off." I asked him, "What would you do now?" Without hesitation he said, "Stop." I responded, "See, I knew you had more power over your behavior than you admit. You just expect too little from yourself. With the right motivation, you can control yourself."

His wife, perhaps for the first time, understood he could control his actions. This helped her to change her expectations of him. The next time he struck her, she went to a shelter for battered women. When he refused to seek help for his problems and continued to blame her for all the problems, she filed for divorce. She had learned to expect more from herself than being a punching bag for her husband.

## A Map to Follow

Map Making is very similar for both those who already are in a relationship and for those who are not. However, there are some important differences to be considered. Often, the alternatives available will be different for couples than for those who are unattached. What might cause you to reconsider whether someone new is right for you, might not be enough reason for ending a long standing relationship.

Let me give you an example of how your relationship status (in or out of a relationship) will affect the various alternatives you will need to consider. If you are an unattached person, with a history of DRS, I would ask you to agree to two conditions: The first condition is to stay out of any serious relationship for some agreed upon time.

The second condition I would ask you to agree to would be to avoid sexual intimacy when you first start serious dating again. We would mutually decide or at least negotiate, how long this abstinence should last.

There are good reasons for both agreements. For the first, my goal is to help the person break his or her DRS patterns. Until these patterns are at least under control, the individual is not ready for another relationship. As you learned earlier, jumping into new relationships quickly, is one sign of DRS. We need time to work on the problems, without the added *excitement* of a new relationship. To borrow a metaphor from the sea, it takes time to develop your sea legs.

As for the latter agreement, it is difficult to look at another person openly and honestly, when you are getting it on with him or her. Sexuality is often confusing enough without attaching to it, the need to learn about another person. If anything, it is human nature to exalt a person you are just starting to have sex with. For those with a history of DRS, this is like playing with matches and gasoline – simultaneously.

If you doubt how confusing sex can make things, I suggest you visit your local library. Ask someone to direct you to the books on human sexuality and the problems related to this subject. When you see the sheer volume of volumes, you will know I am telling you how it really is. You may not want to know this but now you do.

> "You have to accept the fact that part of the sizzle of sex comes from the danger of sex. You can be overpowered." (Camille Paglia – U.S. author, critic, educator. Interview in San Francisco Examiner, July 1991)

Obviously, asking a couple to avoid sex will not go over very well if their relationship already includes sexual intimacy. Changing the rules of the game in this way might lead to more problems with the couple. Instead, I might begin helping each to examine the expectations (maps) they have about their sexuality. Also, what the expectations of the other person are. While not true in all situations, with most couples in distress, their sexual life is distressing too.

Clearly one does not ask a couple to refrain from having a relationship. They are already in one. The exception of course, is if you are asking them to refrain from having multiple, concurrent intimate relationships. This is a subject for a different book and a different author.

## The Map Continues

In the next chapter, I will ask you to answer three questions. Two of these questions will help you to examine your expectations. Your answers will help you to form a much more accurate map. With this map, you will no longer need to wander from place to place – without a plan, relying on luck.

With the knowledge you have acquired through the previous chapters, you are almost where you want to be. What you will learn from your answers to the three questions will allow you to create a successful map to follow. It will not be too difficult to create your new map. By listing your expectations and eliminating the irrational, unrealistic ones, you will be well on your way.

When you begin to add in reasonable expectations, your map really takes shape. As you answer Questions Two and Three, you can make your map very accurate – a map you can follow with more ease. As an additional inducement to do the work required, let me offer this: Your answers will help you to quickly know what kind of map other people have. This knowledge will make your life easier.

For the reader who is in a relationship, this information can help you have a better sense of what is possible and what is not. This knowledge can help you approach your Significant Other in new ways. When we change our approaches to another person, we often get different results. I have seen many relationships dramatically improve, when individuals were willing to examine and change their expectations.

For the reader who is not now in a committed relationship, this chapter can put you on a new path. This path will be built on what is realistic, rather than what leads you to more unhappiness and failure. Of course, I am assuming you are also putting into practice what you have learned and experienced from earlier chapters.

With your new map, your only remaining task will be to actually do something based on your map. You must take action. I do not mean you are to wait for someone else to act or change. You must put into practice those things you have been learning. Until you do, you are simply wishing. "If wishes were horses then beggars would ride." (Unknown).

Several months ago, I was having a friendly debate about the proliferation of Twelve Step Programs. After stating several concerns, I finished with this: The original program was called Twelve Steps – Not Twelve Insights, or Twelve Understandings, or Twelve New Feelings. It was called Twelve Steps because Bill

W (the founder) demanded that people actually do something – take specific steps. "An ounce of action is worth a ton of theory." Friedrich Engels (1820-95).

To paraphrase President John F. Kennedy: Stop asking your relationship to do everything for you. Instead, ask what you (and your mate, if you are in a relationship) can do to make your relationship better.

## Points to Remember

1. Without benefit of a plan, we are destined to wander from place to place. We are leaving our fate to fate, luck and fortune. This may be fine for betting on Roulette. It is not fine if you want a successful relationship.

2. Our expectations are not necessarily based on reality. Instead, our expectations may be built on our inner maps. To improve our chance of having successful relationships, we must be willing to examine and often change our expectations. This results in the creation of new, more realistic maps.

3. Unrealistic and unreasonable expectations are the cause of most of our disappointments and unhappiness. Until you change your inner map, you will continue to get what you have always gotten.

4. By making a new map, based on expectations, which are reasonable, you will act in new ways. When you act differently, it often causes others to respond to you in new ways.

5. You must take action! Knowing is not enough. Until you take action, you are simply being a *legend* in your own mind. This may make you feel better for a short time. It will not be too long before you are experiencing what you have always experienced. To change this, you must practice what you have been learning.

## Compass Directions:

*. . . . I believe that each one of us has within, all the tools and solutions necessary for a more effective life. We sometimes just need some help in knowing where to look. We often spend too much time and energy trying to figure out were other people are. A compass has 360 – degrees, and if we do not know where we are, we have 359 chances out of 360 to go where we don't want to be in the first place.*

**Steven Heller, Ph.D.** (b. 1939), *Monsters and Magical Sticks: There's No Such Thing As Hypnosis? (1987)*

CHAPTER 17

# *Maps To Go*

As I promised in Chapter 16, Map Making 101, you will soon get to answer the three questions I alluded to. The assignment will be a little tricky for you. This is because by the time you get to the questions, you will already know a lot about how to answer them. In spite of this knowledge, I want you to base your answers on what you believed before you read this and the previous chapter.

## FB – Self-Absorbed

To help you with your assignment, I want to give you a case to study. This case will be a good review of some issues I have previously talked about. It will also give you examples of Unrealistic Expectations and Self-Absorption. With these examples, answering the three questions will be easier for you.

FB fit many criteria of Destructive Relationship Syndrome. Her previous relationships had ended badly and she found herself repeating her relationship mistakes. She often jumped into a relationship quickly and without thinking (Too Fast on the Draw). Sometimes, she began a relationship immediately after she or the guy had just ended another relationship (On the Rebound).

In some relationships, she played the Crutchie and often the role of Patient, too. In a few situations, she reversed roles and played the Crutch or Doctor. The men she picked always had a history of being unable to maintain intimacy. As she described it,

"I can't seem to find a man to have a loving relationship with that will last. I am looking for a life partner but my relationships never last."

When she arrived for her first session, she was very absorbed with her fears and problems. She told me she was on medication for depression. Also, that her life was not working very well for her. Her present relationship was filled with chaos and it was on a downward path. She had moved out of the apartment she had shared with her Significant Other, Tom. She moved because she could no longer tolerate all the strife. Even though she moved out, they continued to see each other. FB still hoped that this relationship could be fixed.

When she and Tom got together, they spent their time talking about the problems of the relationship. These talks usually deteriorated into arguments about all the problems in their relationship. This led them both to feel more upset and frustrated, than before they had talked.

Yet, she and Tom agreed, they would not resolve all the issues unless they talked about them. They had been doing so for the past three years. During this period, their relationship had become more filled with stress and problems. Neither could understand why things had not improved. "After all, we always talk about things. They should get better," said FB.

During our first session, I asked FB to put aside all problem talk for one week. She was to tell Tom it was an assignment I had given her. Instead of problem talk, she was to act cheerful and talk about what was going on in the rest of the world. Also, I asked her to become an amateur reporter. This meant I wanted her to listen to other people and to ask them questions.

My purpose was to help her move away from her self-absorption. This condition was one major reason her relationships did not work. From what she said about Tom, he was also self-absorbed. When just one person is self-absorbed, a relationship will experience trouble. Two self-absorbed people create real havoc.

An unknown sage said, "A self-absorbed person is not available for a meaningful relationship. They are already committed to someone else." With her degree of self-absorption, there was no room for anything else. If Tom was even only nearly as self-absorbed, the situation was not going to improve easily.

During this session, I gave her the Question of the Year. She answered by picking answer number one: "Completely free from stress and unhappiness." I had her read what the studies had concluded. FB was shocked at the correct answer. In her mind, until all her fears were gone and her problems solved, she could not be happy. These are the things she focused on.

According to FB, her biggest fear was of being alone – particularly of going anywhere by herself. She was aware how limiting her fear was and she wanted to change this pattern. FB realized this fear made her cling to men and they got tired of this very quickly. Also, some of her friends were tired of her calling or showing up because she was left alone and felt fearful.

During our first session, I used some techniques to help her lower her level of fear. Next, I asked her to go out to dinner by herself, at least twice in the coming week. While at dinner alone, she was to keep a written log about her thoughts and her feelings.

To encourage her, I told her this assignment would help me to help her relationship. Also, I agreed to meet with her and Tom, but only if she carried out this assignment. However, I said we would not have a joint session for at least three weeks. I believed it would take this long before she was ready.

FB carried out this assignment and others as I gave them to her. Within a few weeks, her attitude, demeanor and outlook on life had noticeably improved. We began to work more directly on her DRS and the problems within her current relationship. It became clear to me, she did not really know what she could realistically expect from any relationship. From what I heard from her, no living person could come close to meeting her expectations.

Not only did FB have unrealistic expectations, she also confused what a person must do for herself, with what a relationship could do for her. She expected a relationship to provide her with the kind of security only she could give herself. FB believed that being in a relationship would magically give her the ability to have a happy life.

Many individuals and couples I have worked with have had the same kind of confusion. It seems that Destructive Relationship Syndrome is often chained to unrealistic and confused expectations. Where you find one, you will find the other.

## Relationship Questions

During the first joint session, I asked FB and Tom to do some homework. They were to answer the three questions I was about to ask them. Also, they were not to discuss their answers with each other until we all met again. I suggested they take part of the coming week to think about the questions. Then, they could write out their answers. They were to write everything each could think of, which might be important, in the answering of these questions.

The first question was: What do I want and expect from a relationship? Second question: What do I expect from the other person? The third question: What are my responsibilities and obligations to my relationship? (Now you know what the questions are. Soon, it will be your turn to answer them).

FB arrived for the next session without Tom. He had something to do, which he thought was too important to miss. (I would like you to draw your own inferences from this). It would be several weeks before I would get Tom's answers. When I did get them, they looked like they were thrown together while riding on a roller coaster. At the least, I could see, very little effort had gone into his answers – but I digress.

The answers FB gave me were very interesting. I will focus on her answers to Question One. One answer she came up with was: "A relationship should make us take responsibility for ourselves and our lives as a couple and individually."

A relationship cannot do these things. Both people should already be responsible for their own lives before they are even ready to consider entering a relationship. If either is not being responsible, a relationship will not change this. I believe that a relationship will make each person more likely to avoid becoming a responsible person.

FB believed being in a relationship, would compel both to become responsible people. This would be about the same as expecting an alcoholic to no longer drink because he got into a relationship. I know there are those who believe this but studies clearly show it is not true.

One woman I worked with, knew her boyfriend would stop gambling if they got married. He would be *compelled* to become a responsible person. She *knew* marriage matured people. In spite of my warnings or perhaps because of them, they got married. The first thing he did was to sell most of their wedding presents. He took the proceeds and gambled with them.

Another answer FB had was, "To be monogamous and committed to the relationship." Here too, she confused personal responsibility and character for what a relationship can do.

Remember, in my introduction to this book, I said that a relationship is not a living thing but is made up of the people in it. If you choose to be in a relationship with someone who has a history of promiscuity, why would you expect he would magically stop because he is now in a relationship? Why would you be surprised when he continued to do what he has always done?

She wrote, "I want a man who is bright, a good cook, with a good personality, someone who has good manners and is basically polite." While all these are desirable qualities to find in someone, not one has anything to do with what a relationship can give you. Rather, they all have to do with what you might want to find in the person you wish to have a relationship with.

If a person is kind, polite and has good manners, these traits will probably continue. Where the person lacks any or all these, this condition will probably continue too. People bring their good and bad habits with them, wherever they go. This includes when they enter into a relationship. The exception to this would be where he or she is willing to make personal changes. Other than this exception, there are no exceptions.

Here are two more answers she gave: "I want us both to strive toward being vulnerable with each other by being secure within ourselves." and "I want us to love and trust ourselves, so we can love and trust each other." Again, a relationship can do none of these for you.

If you think about the last two answers FB gave, you will see how they are about personal goals. While each person might like to achieve these things, they are not something a relationship can achieve for you. Only by individual work can one achieve individual goals. A healthy relationship will encourage each person to achieve such goals and this makes it easier. But, each person will still have to do the work.

Now, look at the following by FB: "I expect the relationship to make my life more comfortable. With both of us working for common goals, it should be easier to get more of what we want."

If you recall, earlier in this book, I said a relationship should be an easier way to live. I gave examples about how a good relationship often makes things easier and more comfortable for both. FB's last two expectations fit this concept. To me, both are realistic expectations about what we can get from a relationship.

While it can be said it is up to each person to make his own life comfortable, a good relationship can contribute to this goal. Many studies have shown that individuals within a good relationship often live longer, enjoy better health, live more comfortably and have a higher degree of satisfaction for life. Also, couples usually have better financial underpinnings than do individuals.

If FB had said she wanted her relationship to be the kind that allowed her to develop her skills and talents, this would be a realistic expectation. Good relationships allow and encourage personal growth. Bad relationships usually interfere with these desires. The stress and strain of a bad relationship often leave little time or energy for personal improvement.

Again, we must remember a relationship is just the sum of its part(ner)s. We have little or no chance of getting anything reasonable, if either or both of the partners are not handling life well. Where this is the situation, the relationship will suffer, as will the people in the relationship.

## Your Turn

It is now time for you to answer the questions I have been talking about. Let me review them again. The first question is: What do I expect from a relationship?

Think about your expectations and wants. Be thorough and include everything you can think of. I do not want you to be concerned if the expectations are possible or reasonable.

An honest look at what you really have believed, will help you to make a better map. Just use your common sense and say what needs to be said. Ralph Waldo Emerson (1803-82) said, "Nothing astonishes men so much as common sense and plain dealing."

Let me give you some general examples. Many people believe (expect) that they will never be lonely while in a relationship. This belief is guaranteed to lead to disappointment. It is human to feel lonely once in awhile – in a relationship or not. A person who has this expectation, will begin to wonder what is wrong when she feels lonely, while in a relationship. None the less, if it is something you have expected, write it down.

Here is another common expectation about being in a relationship. "I will always feel loved and complete because I am in a relationship." These expectations are doomed to be unmet. Outside yourself, nothing can make you feel complete! As for always feeling loved, this will depend on the quality of your relationship and your interpretation of things. Just like feeling lonely, sometimes we all feel unloved or unappreciated. A relationship cannot remove these conditions.

What if you believe your relationship should have lots of romance in it? This is achievable albeit not perfectly so. If both want this and are willing to act in ways which encourage romance, you will succeed. You may not always succeed but you will often. When people want a relationship to be romantic, they can shape it to be this way.

Next, answer question two: What do I expect from my Significant Other or Potential S.O.?

I have worked with many people who expected their S.O. would never be attracted to another person. Also, many people think their Significant Other will never even look at another man or woman. If you think either of these things, be sure you include them in your answers. These will become areas for you to examine later.

During our journey through life, we will all be attracted to other people. To expect someone to be free of those feelings is to expect what is not possible. Also, it is common and human to occasionally glance at someone we find to be attractive. Of course, you can expect the other person to refrain from acting on his or her attractions. This expectation is not only possible but prudent too.

Here are two more things people often expect of their mates. Many have learned to expect their mates will always agree with them. If this fits you, write it down. Also, I have worked with many people who believe their mates should know what they are thinking, without the need for actually saying anything.

Both expectations are impossible for anyone to achieve. People will always have some differences. What a boring world it would be if we were alike. I would say that some differences add good spice to any relationship.

As for always knowing what someone thinks, this is beyond unrealistic – it comes close to an irrational belief. (My Gypsy Fortune Telling License expired and I have never renewed it). Although you now know the truth about these two expectations, write them down, if you believe in them.

If you expect someone to be thoughtful, considerate and polite, include these in your answers. These seem to me, to be realistic and appropriate things to expect from another person. You may expect another person to keep their word, be on time and follow up on what they commit to. Write these down and pat yourself on the back. These are appropriate expectations.

What if you expect the other person never to flirt? Is this a reasonable or an unreasonable expectation? This is a trick question because there is not a clear-cut answer. Let us say you are attracted to someone who loves to flirt. You think it is cute – until you decide this is a person with whom you want to be involved. Now, the two of you begin moving toward creating a committed relationship.

Simultaneously, you expect her to magically see the light and to stop her flirting. Why should she? Have you even discussed this with her? Has she freely agreed to stop flirting? If not and you will not or cannot accept this behavior, you will need to make a decision. You may need to decide this person is not someone you should become involved with.

If you decide to continue with her, you know what you can expect. The only way you will not know, is if you choose our old friend *"denial."* You are the only one who knows what you really believe and are willing to accept.

Anyway, be as complete as possible listing what you expect from someone else. Until you know what you expect, you will still be relying on fate to lead you. Once you see what your expectations are, it will become easier to decide which ones make sense and which do not. This also helps you to know which expectations you need to change because they are unrealistic.

Now, I want you to answer Question Three. To me, Question Three is the most important of the questions. "What are my responsibilities and obligations to the other person and my relationship?"

We all need to understand this important idea. To be in a relationship is to accept responsibility. Each person has obligations to the other person and to the relationship too. It does not matter if it is hard to do or we do not feel like doing it. We must do what is right – what we have promised to do.

To have expectations of someone else, while giving ourselves permission to act anyway we want or feel like acting, is to invite disaster into our lives.

I will go further: There are no excuses, short of a true life and death situation for not keeping our commitments and promises. Without character all else matters not. To attempt building a relationship while giving up your character is to build a house on quick sand. You will expend much effort and what you build will sink!

Character is the basis of happiness and happiness the sanction of character. George Santayana (1863-1952),

U.S. philosopher, poet. The Life of Reason, ch. 9, "Reason in Common Sense" (1905-6).

## I Don't Want To

I just talked to a woman who was upset because her husband said he was moving out. While he is at least equally responsible for the problems, I want to focus on her part. It relates directly to the subject of a person's responsibilities and obligations to a mate and to a relationship.

During our first session, she made a commitment to me to follow certain instructions. Together, we wrote these out and talked in detail about the reasons for each instruction. Of even more importance, she had made several promises to her husband about how she would comport herself within the coming two weeks. Based on these promises, he had agreed to work on their marriage and seek therapy for himself.

Several days later, she called me in a state of panic. Her husband had packed his bags and moved out. For whatever her reasons, she had given herself excuses to break every promise she had made but one. When I told her she had acted irresponsibly, she said, "Why should I have to be the one who has to be responsible. I shouldn't have to keep my promises if it's hard for me."

When I told her she could not hope to save her marriage this way, she got angry. "You're supposed to make me feel better. Why should I have to feel bad just because I couldn't keep my promises? I wanted to try but I kept forgetting,"

## Responsibility

> "We are responsible for actions performed in response to circumstances for which we are not responsible." Allan Massie (b. 1938), British author. Etienne, in A Question of Loyalties, (1989). Columbia University Press.©1993.

Anyway, your answers to question three are very important to you. For a relationship to be successful, each person must be able to accept the obligations and responsibilities which are part of a relationship. However, you can only assure that you and you alone will accept these obligations and responsibilities. You cannot make another person accept obligations or responsibilities.

Accepting obligations and responsibilities means you must have character. According to the Random House Webster's College Dictionary, Character:

> "refers esp. to the moral qualities and ethical standards that make up the inner nature of a person." Also "Moral or ethical strength. A description of a person's attributes, traits, or abilities."

Let me be explicit: You need to have or develop the character needed, if you hope to have a successful relationship with anyone. Also, you will never have self-esteem and self-respect, unless you are someone with character. Here is another view of Character:

> "The best index to a person's character is (a) how he treats people who can't do him any good, and (b) how he treats people who can't fight back." Abigail Van Buren (b. 1918), U.S. columnist.

Former President, Ronald Reagan, had a lighter view of the subject of character:

> "You can tell a lot about a fellow's character by his way of eating jelly beans." (Columbia Dictionary of Quotations – 1993.)

## Points to Remember

1. Self-absorbed people are not available for a relationship. They are too preoccupied to be available for anyone.
2. Destructive Relationship Syndrome guarantees the presence of unrealistic and confused expectations. These types of expectations make all relationships difficult and painful.
3. You need to learn about your expectations. Make sure you answer the following questions: What do I expect from a relationship? What do I expect from the other person? What are my obligations and responsibilities to the other person and the relationship?
4. Without personal character, you cannot expect any relationship to succeed. If either or both lack this trait, there will be trouble, until character is developed.
5. Another reason to develop personal character is to have self-esteem and self-respect. These two things cannot exist without the presence of character.

## Chapter 18

# *Sculpting Your Map*

When creating a sculpture, the artist knows it is what he chisels away, which decides what the sculpture will finally be. This is true when you are creating a new map to follow. The unreasonable expectations you chisel away, will help your new map take shape.

The process of sculpting your map will include your answers to the Three Questions found in the last chapter. You must begin chiseling away expectations, which your personal history suggests, you have little or no chance of obtaining. The same must be done for those expectations you recognize as unrealistic or even irrational.

I know it is hard for most of us to admit we have unrealistic or irrational expectations. We often go to extreme lengths to prove our expectations are valid. Still, we must find a way to admit the truth about our expectations, if we are serious about creating a new map which will lead us to better destinations.

"Our systems, perhaps, are nothing more than an unconscious apology for our faults – a gigantic scaffolding whose object is to hide from us our favorite sin." Henri-frédéric Amiel (1821-81), Swiss philosopher, poet. Journal Intime, 1882, Columbia University Press. Copyright©1993 by Columbia University Press.

## Maps For One or Two

What you do with your new map will be affected by your relationship status. An unattached person will not need to *educate* another person about the new map, which is being created. For the unattached person, the effort should be aimed toward finding someone whose map is compatible. Also, as your new map begins to take shape you will find yourself changing expectations and the type of individual you are looking for.

If you are in a relationship, you will have the task of helping the other person to understand the new map you are creating. Unless you are going to end your relationship, you do not have the option of finding a person whose map is more compatible with yours. This means, after you have created your map, you still have work to do.

You will need to help your mate understand your new set of expectations. Also, you need to clearly define your obligations and responsibilities and those you have to your Significant Other. When you create a new map, you are changing the rules which have been governing your situation. While these changes are intended to improve your life, you still need to let your S.O. know what you are doing. Rule changes can be unsettling – at least for a short period.

At first glance, it may seem as if the unattached person has an easier task than does the person in a relationship. Well, it is easier and it is not. While the attached person has an added responsibility, she or he will get feedback quickly. The responses we receive from another person, can help us to check how our maps are working. Of course, we must be willing to listen to and consider another person's opinions.

The unattached person is freed from the task of updating their Significant Other. However, there is a price the unattached person will have to pay. If you are unattached, you will not have anyone to help point out when you are deviating from your map. You will not get any feedback nor will you have someone who tries to encourage you in your quest. This can make the task of map making more difficult for you.

## The Slob – Attached or Not

Following is a scenario I have had to work with often. How I have proceeded with this situation has been shaped by the relationship status of the individuals I have been working with. Although the complaint might be the same, I approach an unattached person differently than I would a couple. I have named the complaint I will now talk about – The Slob.

For illustrative purposes, I will define The Slob as someone who does not clean up after himself or herself. This person leaves clothes on the floor and furniture and seldom cleans up after eating. The exception might be when he or she runs out of dishes or has company coming. The Slob does not take good care of nearly anything. This person seldom puts something back and does not seem to mind lots of dirt, or at least lots of mess.

Let me assume you are married to or have been in a relationship of long standing with The Slob. You have talked about your unhappiness with The Slob's lack of neatness. These talks may have included threatening, bribing, pleading and reasoning. You may have even tried silence. Your efforts have produced only one consistent result – no change. By now, you are filled with resentment, disappointment and unhappiness. These attributes do not enhance your relationship.

What can you do? Only one thing – if you wish to preserve your relationship. You must change what you expect when it comes to slovenly behavior. Ending a marriage or long standing relationship because of this behavior is a very drastic solution.

Unless there are more areas which cause you real discomfort, you will need to accept this is just the way he or she is. By changing what you expect from your mate, you will have less reason to stay upset with The Slob. By going beyond your feelings of upset, your relationship will benefit.

I am not suggesting you learn to love the slovenly behavior. What I am suggesting is to stop driving yourself crazy about what you cannot change. Here is an idea – find an acceptable solution. That is what I did with the couple you are going to read about next.

## Married to a Slob

This couple fit the "He is such a slob" scenario. Judy was what I call a *neatness freak*. Her husband Jack was not even close to being neat. Jack would drop things where he took them off and would not pick up after himself. If he happened to make his lunch, the kitchen would look like it had been hit by a small bomb. He even left dirty clothes in the trunk of his car.

How he came to leave dirty clothes in his car is a long story and not essential to this case. One thing I found interesting is sometimes, he managed to put some of his wife's clothes in his trunk too. Often, her clothes would stay in the trunk of his car for several weeks, without her knowledge. To put it mildly, this did not please her in the slightest way.

This couple had fought about this problem for several years. Often, the arguments became extremely intense. Then, he would promise to mend his ways. His commitment to better behavior would sometimes last as long as three days. With the help of a Marriage–Family–Therapist, they had even signed a contract about this issue. Even with this contract, the results were not worth all the effort and hassles they experienced.

Besides fighting about his slovenly behavior, Jack and Judy had begun to fight about the contract too. She was angry with him because he broke his word. He was angry with her because he had not wanted to sign the contract in the first place. They were now spending as much time fighting about the broken contract as they were about his being a slob.

According to her, he was being a slob because he did not really care about her feelings. Her position was simple: If he cared about me he would change this behavior. (Reality or expectations?) Since he refused to change, he did not really love her.

He believed she picked on him because she did not have any respect for him. (Expectations or reality?) "A woman who respects her man would never pick on him. She always picks on me, so she doesn't respect me." Jack repeated this litany several times during our first few sessions.

They did manage to agree about a few things. One area of agreement was that they were both very angry. Also, they agreed that if only the other would admit being wrong, things would be better. Another area of agreement was that they could not go on this way much longer. They wanted to save their marriage.

They also agreed that their relationship was a good one, at least basically. Because of this, they were willing to try anything reasonable that could help them stay together. Both said this issue was about the only issue which caused serious problems in their marriage. Each believed that if only the other would be reasonable (give in), the problem would go away. To me, it appeared each was waiting for the other to make the first move (change).

My first task was to help them each to examine the expectations, which were causing this set of problems. He expected her to wake up and stop being so concerned about how neat things were. Also, he expected her to show respect by never finding any fault with him.

She, of course, expected him to see the light and give up being a slob. To her, this was one major way of showing he cared about her. However, he was not going to see the light, nor was he going to easily give up being a slob.

It took a few sessions before I could get them to examine their expectations. When each realized it was their expectations which caused problems for the relationship, each agreed to approach things differently. As they did this, there was a significant drop in the level of acrimony.

I helped them to see how they attached emotional results to the actions of the other. She was able to understand and accept that his behavior had nothing to do with his caring about her. Instead, he was just a slob. That was the way he had always been.

He came to realize she was a neatness freak and that is how she had always been. This behavior had nothing to do with respecting him. Also, he agreed it was OK that she did not respect his being a slob. This was not the same as not respecting him. He admitted he did not respect himself for being a slob. To date, he had not found any reason to change the behavior. No one had ever been able to get him to stop being a slob.

My solution was to have them hire a local teenager to come in and pick things up. The husband agreed to pay for this in return for the wife agreeing to "get off and stay off my back." Was this a perfect or even outstanding solution? No! But, ending an otherwise good marriage over this issue would have been stupid.

At first, they had some resistance to what I had suggested. After I pointed out that if they divorced, the lawyers would get at least one third of all their assets, they became more open-minded. Magically, they realized hiring someone was a small price to pay. Until then, I guess no one had helped them have a good reason to find a solution to this problem.

## Not Attached

For an unattached person, there are different criteria to consider. If you begin to date The Slob, the issue is: Can you accept this behavior? You will need to look at yourself honestly before you can answer this question.

If you discover you really cannot handle this type of behavior, admit it. Then, you must move on. There is very little chance The Slob will see the light and change. Finding someone who is not a slob will be easier for you. If you continue with this person, after knowing you cannot accept the behavior, you are the problem.

If, after knowing you cannot accept the problem, you continue to date this person, he or she will take your apparent acceptance as real acceptance. Then if you demand change, it will seem as if you have changed the rules of the game after the game has started. This is a good way to get someone really angry with you.

Too often, people in love or attracted to each other, are convinced that the things they do not like will change. All they have to do is live together, or get engaged, or get married. This is similar to expecting a Zebra to turn his stripes into dots because he sees another Zebra he thinks is a fox (a little slang for a good-looking female Zebra).

People do change. However, if someone's behavior really bugs you, it will be easier for you to find someone else then to get this person to change. This is why an unattached person has an advantage over someone who is already in a relationship. Finding a more suitable partner is much easier than ending an existing relationship. Also, it is far less painful, costly or time consuming.

I am not suggesting you dump a potential Significant Other because of little quirks. You are not going to find someone who is perfect. The perfect people have all moved to another world. We must settle for real people and real people have flaws and behaviors about which we may not always be thrilled.

## Really Bad Behavior

Of course, if your potential mate is a bank robber, mugger or other type felon, you need to make a decision. Based on his history, if he is not going to change, you need to develop a very realistic set of expectations: He is a crook and always will be. It is time for you to examine what your expectations are and ask, "What in the hell am I doing in this situation? I need to get out."

It does not matter if he has other good qualities or that you love him. These kinds of behaviors will only lead to grief. His other good qualities and your love will not change anything.

If you are dating this kind of character, you need to stop – right now! Your expectations are irrational. Until you see concrete evidence, which demonstrates a real change, you need to run and run fast – in another direction. What I have just said is true for lessor unacceptable behavior. A relationship will no more cause someone to change than lighting candles will.

A few months ago, a woman came to see me. She had married a guy who had a history of being promiscuous. He also lied about nearly everything and did not keep his word. It was so bad, she could not trust him at all.

I asked her what she expected me to do. She said, "I am really upset that he keeps doing these things. He promised he would change if we got married. You need to help me learn what I can do to make him change. He says I expect too much from him."

I told her that when I applied for the job of God, it was already taken. Then I explained to her that he has proven, beyond a doubt, he would not change. When I told her that I believed he did not have character or ethics, she got angry with me. She insisted he wanted to change.

I asked her why he had not come with her or made an appointment for himself. "He does not believe in therapy or asking anyone for help. Besides, he says I am the one with all the problems."

If you are in a long standing relationship or married to someone who is like the person I have just described, you have big problems. Unless he or she is willing to get professional help, nothing will ever change. Even with competent help, the road will be filled with pot holes. Some of these pot holes will be deep enough to shake things up. If the person is not willing to get help, you need to get out of the relationship. There is no other reasonable alternative.

If you are unattached and you are attracted to a person who is promiscuous, breaks his word, is wasteful with money, lies, etc. face facts. He or she will not change merely because you enter a relationship. It is your expectations which are out of whack. You can try to put off facing the truth or pretend things will change. Sure, right after someone names me the winner of $50,000,000 in the Clearing House Give Away.

## Obligations and Duties

In Chapter 17, I said of the Three Questions, the third was the most important: What are your responsibilities and obligations to another person and your relationship? I cannot emphasize too strongly, how important personal responsibility is. To have expectations without responsibility is to ask for something without giving anything of value.

"A task becomes a duty from the moment you suspect it to be an essential part of that integrity which alone entitles a man to assume responsibility." Dag Hammarskjöld (1905-61), Swedish statesman, Secretary-General of U.N. Markings, "Night is Drawing Nigh" (1963; written 1955).

When I talk about responsibility and obligations, I am talking about having character. Let me again refer to the definition of character according to The American Heritage Dictionary of the English Language, Character: Moral or ethical strength. A description of a person's attributes, traits, or abilities.

When a person lacks character, all else will matter little. You can neither give someone else character, nor can you get character from a book, class or pill. If you are a parent, you can help your children develop character but they too, will need to find it for themselves. This trait is like Gravity – Character keeps everything from slipping away.

Because the subject of character is so important, I want to give you several examples to consider. If you want to have character, you must be honest and tell the truth. You must keep your word and follow through on what you commit to. Another person is never to be treated as if he or she is a garbage can. This means you cannot dump on someone because you have had a bad day or you are mad at someone else.

At all times you must treat others in respectful ways. I am not saying you have to respect someone – only that you act with respect. This is even more true when it comes to how you treat your Significant Other. Can you be kind, even when you are angry? Are you willing to show caring even when your mate is out of line? If you are to have character, you need to learn how to do all of these things.

Because there are so many areas to consider, you will need to exercise your mind. You will need to think! I want you to consider your responsibilities in areas such as communication, keeping your promises, being productive, learning about another person, being reliable and handling your financial affairs.

What about sexuality? Have you ever really looked at what your responsibilities and obligations to another person are? You need to do so. The subject of sexuality often causes problems for couples. I am still amazed at the couples who have no idea that they have some responsibility for love making and sensuality itself.

Throughout this book, I have introduced you to methods and techniques for personal change. As one example, you learned about my Four Steps Communication method, along with the importance of listening and asking questions. It is your responsibility to practice these things until they become second nature. You may have reasons and excuses which allow you to avoid doing so. If this describes you, then you are not showing good character.

It is only by adding your responsibilities and obligations to your map that it can be accurate. You will make it easier on yourself because you will know what you need to do. Also, your map helps you to know what another person's map is about. This will allow you to know if the other person has character. If they do not, are you willing to settle for a relationship with someone you cannot ever believe or count on?

## Admirable or Not

Here is an informal assignment for you. You can do it either in your head or on paper. I want you to think about all the people you have met, whom you have admired or respected. Now, what qualities did these people have?

I know you will see commonalities if you look. It is like examining successful business people. You will find they have core similarities, even if there are differences. The same is true with people you admire.

Next, remember several people you did not admire or respect. Be careful. I am not talking about liking or disliking someone. You must limit your search to those you did not admire or respect. What qualities did they have which you did not respect? You might want to focus on what qualities they did not have. You can do this by comparing this group to the first.

While I run the risk of oversimplifying, here is what I believe you will find. The people whom you admire will show character. They will keep their word, have ethics and accept responsibility for themselves. While there may be many subtle behaviors also present, keeping their word, ethics and accepting responsibility will stand out.

When you examine those whom you do not admire or respect, you will see an absence of character. Often, there will be a refusal to accept any responsibility for their own actions. This group of people will be expert at the art of excuse making. Often, their word can best be described as fluid.

It is up to you, which group you choose to emulate. It is my hope you will do more of what the first group does and much less of what the second group does. You will benefit as will your relationships. This can only lead to a happier and more successful life. This is a pretty good reward for taking time to develop good character.

## Points to Remember

1. To create a new map, which will be more accurate, we must be willing to chisel away our unreasonable expectations.
2. If you are in a relationship, you must talk about what you are doing with your Significant Other. You need to keep you S.O. apprised of how you are changing your expectations. By making a new map, you are changing the old rules. Do not expect your S.O. to read your mind.
3. If you are unattached, you will need to test what you are doing. Also, as you eliminate unrealistic expectations, go slowly with developing new expectations. Find a friend you trust to test them out on.
4. People do not easily change their longstanding habits or behavior. If you expect someone will change because you enter a relationship with him or her, you will be disappointed. People change when they decide they want to. Even then, it takes time and effort.
5. Your expectations should help you to develop personal character. A person who lacks character is similar to a Hollywood movie set: All show and no substance – merely a facade.
6. If your (potential) mate lacks character, you need to reconsider your position. There is very little chance he or she will ever be willing to change. It is more likely that the behavior you do not like will occur more often as time goes on.

CHAPTER 19

# *Leave Taking*

Together, we have looked at and discussed a myriad of issues and ideas that pertain to the subject of relationships. I know that the concept of Destructive Relationship Syndrome is new to you. Because of this, I know it will take time for you to be able to assimilate all the material I have offered in this book.

Throughout this journey, I have tried to keep in mind that I am both your host and your guest. I am your host because I have led you on this journey which I have created for you. Simultaneously, I am your guest, because you have invited me, through this book, into your thoughts and beliefs. In many ways, the tasks of being a host and the obligations of being a guest are quite different.

As your host, I have a responsibility to make the event or journey (this book) an interesting experience. Also, it is my obligation to include enough within the event, both to entertain and to inform you. The event should not be over so quickly, that the guests feel rushed. Yet, the event should not last so long that the invitees become bored or fatigued. Finding this balance is for me, a difficult task.

In the role of a guest, I have a different set of tasks. I must not rush out of the event as if I could not wait to go. This would be rude. Yet, I must not stay so long, as to wear out my welcome. While I am your guest, I must respect that it is I who run the risk of intruding on your time. Finding a balance, is a daunting task, at least for me.

While there are many collateral issues I could introduce and areas I could add to, the time is quickly coming to say my goodbyes. Bear with me for just a short while longer. There are a few things I need to say before I close. To me, these things are important for you to consider. That is why I am willing to risk overstaying my welcome.

## Best Wart Forward

A school counselor referred a twelve-year old boy to me. This boy, whom I will call Tim, was painfully shy. Along with his shyness, he had a few mannerisms, which made him seem very different from his classmates.

Kids being kids, they picked Tim as a target for their verbal insults. Tim responded to these insults with anger. Often, he would scream at his tormentors. This only served to isolate him more. Because he was isolated, it made it easier for the others to single him out. This led to more attacks by them and more angry outbursts by Tim. The beat went on.

Along with the problems Tim was having with his classmates, he had also begun to do poorly with school work. He had become a loner and was without friends. Tim was a very sad young boy. While he did not know it, his way of dealing with the problems made him an easy target. As he became more of a loner, he stood out even more.

I helped Tim learn the Blackboard Technique and to use Flash Cards. Also, I taught him specific methods of responding to the verbal attacks, which I knew would soon defuse the attacks. He was also taught some self-hypnosis to help him be calmer. I showed him ways to use self-hypnosis to become more focused and confident.

Within six sessions, his demeanor and attitude had gone through a complete reversal. He had made friends out of most of his former tormentors. These friends now stood up for him against the few who still saw him as the butt of their jokes. Tim's school work improved (he was very bright) and he was getting along well with his family. He and I were happy with his progress.

One day, Tim walked in for a session, with a very serious look on his face. "Dr. Heller, I really need your help with something that is bothering me" he said. I asked him to tell me about it and I would see what I could do. "I met a girl at school and I really like her. I don't know if she likes me. You told me I have to take chances even when I am afraid, so I asked her to meet me for a movie and pizza. She said yes but I still don't know if she really likes me."

"What kind of help do you want?" I asked. "Teach me what I can do to really impress her. I know you can show me how to talk to her so she will be impressed with me." With as much of a wise countenance as I could muster, I said, "Tim, you must put your best wart forward!"

Tim looked puzzled and said, "Yuck. Why would I do that? Warts are ugly and besides I don't have any." I explained to him I was using a wart as an example (metaphor) and to imagine he did have one. He said, "If I show her my wart, she might not like me. I would rather hide it."

"This is what many people (including adults) think, but it is still the wrong way to do things. Pretend you have a wart and you hide it. Now, this girl seems to like you. You won't know if she likes you for you or for who you are pretending to be. This means you will need to keep hiding the truth from her. And you will always be nervous around her. This is because you will be afraid that she will find out about your secret and not like you anymore," was my response.

Tim said, "What if I show her my wart and she thinks it's ugly and doesn't like me because of it?" I told him this could happen and it would be sad but, "It means she never would have really liked you for you. While it is sad, at least you found out fast. You could have spent lots of time and energy and then found out she wouldn't like you. This way, you find out fast and you can look for someone who will like and accept you."

Then I said, "Here is something else that could happen. You could show her you wart and she could say, "So what. It's no big deal." Now you know she will like you for who you are. Also, she might even say she has warts too. This means she not only likes you, she also trusts you to like her for who she is."

As he got used to it, Tim really liked the idea of Put Your Best Wart Forward. He said some very nice things about how clever I was to figure this out. With some modesty, I told him I was not the first person to figure it out. Other people had figured it out before me. How little did I know how true this was. In fact, it had been figured out hundreds of years ago.

## Old Wisdom

A Hasidic Rabbi, who lived during the seventeenth century, told a story which illustrated Putting Your Best Wart Forward. He told of a revered, admired and honored Rabbi, who passed on the ancient traditions of his people. While he was greatly admired, he was not liked or loved as a person. He knew this and accepted it. Being alone and lonely was the price he paid to be a teacher of his people, or so he believed.

The Rabbi was invited to come to a village and teach to a large congregation. When he was in front of the congregation, he began telling stories of the old ways. As he did so, a memory came into his mind. It was a memory of a time he had acted like a fool – like the ass of a donkey. He pushed the memory away because it would embarrass him to tell this story.

While he continued with his teaching, the memory came flooding back. This time, it was even stronger then before. Being a man of God, he assumed God was asking him to reveal this story. "I am a learned teacher and a respected Rabbi," he thought. "If I tell this story, people will laugh at me. I may lose their respect. However, God must want me to tell it."

With great trepidation, he began to reveal his embarrassing story. As he feared, the congregation laughed upon hearing of his foolish behavior. Then, "they opened their hearts and let me in," he said. From that time on, he was not just respected, he was loved. The people would welcome him into their homes and would share meals with him. This had not happened before *He Put His Best Wart Forward.*

The Hasidic Rabbi also asked, "Why does man build houses with windows and then cover the windows with curtains?" When I ask this of the people I work with, I hear many answers. My answer is, "So that we have choice about how much or little light to allow in." Also, "So we can have choice about whom and when we allow others to look into to our homes."

The Rabbi said (and I paraphrase him,) "We must allow others to look in our windows to see how we really keep our homes, if we want someone to know us. When they see we are all very much alike, they may allow us to look into their homes, so that we may know them."

Today, we are bombarded with commercials, advice, movies, songs and more, which tell us to hide our warts. We are told how to use subterfuge, slight of hand and misstatements so we can fool other people. Does this have anything to do with how disconnected people seem to be from each other?

Experts offer to teach us how to come up with better lines to use to try and pick up (meet) someone. This tells us that an honest response to another person is to be avoided. Avoiding an honest response must be the right thing to do. After all, the experts tell us so.

Within nearly every relationship problem I have ever dealt with, I have found dishonesty. People hide their fears and flaws from those whom they say they love. When dating, it is common for people to go out of their way to give false impressions. Of course we call this making a good impression. Whatever we call it, it is still dishonesty. How can we build a successful, loving relationship on a foundation of dishonesty?

I am not suggesting we act in ways which are not appropriate. Nor am I suggesting we *let it all hang out*. We need to act with character, style and grace as much as possible. This does not preclude telling the truth nor does it require you to hide your warts. If done with discretion, self-disclosure can often lead to more intimacy between people.

> "If ever a man and his wife, or a man and his mistress, who pass nights as well as days together, absolutely lay aside all good breeding, their intimacy will soon degenerate into a coarse familiarity, infallibly productive

of contempt or disgust." Lord Chesterfield (1694-1773), English statesman, man of letters. Letter, 3 Nov. 1749.

Also, I do not mean gratuitously offering to show your warts or going out of your way to find an excuse to expose them. Instead, I am suggesting you develop a willingness to expose them in the appropriate contexts and circumstances. I think you will like the results. You will make it easier for other people to know you. This is very important for the kind of relationships we all are attempting to create.

## Guru or Not?

There is another area of confusion I want to talk about. It is about the Gurus who preach Instant Cures, whether they be known as "Instant Success" or "Instant Power" or any other such misleading titles. Here too, we are being constantly bombarded with messages about gaining "instant" this, that or something else. Often, the only thing that is "instant" is the large amounts of money the purveyors of "Instant Cures" make.

Some of these self-appointed Gurus claim to have all the answers to all your problems. "If only you will practice X, you will free yourself from all your doubts. . . . I will show you how to succeed in every one of your endeavors. . . . You can have absolute confidence in every situation." These and even more outlandish claims are made every day, in every media. What are we to believe?

To answer this last question, I again wish to look at the teachings of some early philosophers and teachers. From several of these, I have created the following metaphor. It is based on my understanding of what these specific teachings offered to us.

During a time of great upheaval, sometime in the mid sixteen hundreds, people were looking for guidance. Then, as now, many men rose up and proclaimed themselves to be teachers (Gurus) and leaders. They claimed to have the knowledge needed to survive the troubled times. Also, magic being much in vogue, many claimed to be able to teach this magic. How was the average person to know which one to believe?

The elders were asked, "How are we to know who is truly a teacher and who is a trickster?" At first, the elders had no answer for the people. They debated this question for several days. After long, careful deliberation and debate, they arrived at what they believed to be an answer to this question.

The people were called together and the elders appeared. "We have discovered how you may know the true teacher from the man who would trick you. You must ask of any self-professed teacher three questions: Will you help me to be free from all fear? Will you show me how to expel all evil thoughts and temptations? Can you teach me how to prosper at whatever endeavors I choose?"

"If any man says yes to any of these questions, run from him. He is a false prophet. Part of life is to prevail in spite of our fears and the fears we will experience during our lives. Life also includes bad thoughts and temptations, above which we must struggle to rise."

"Lastly, look amongst you and see if you can find one man who has never suffered from disappointment or failure. If such a man exists, surely he is not a mere man. We mortals will fall, get up, stumble and fall again. It is our will to achieve which creates the desire to risk the failure. This will to achieve also propels us to rise when we have stumbled."

While my metaphor is not as elegant as the ones the ancient philosophers might have used, it does make my point clear. Life includes struggles, mistakes, failures and sometimes, some pretty dumb thinking. However, these things are just ruts in the road. They are not what our total lives are about.

I have already pointed out with The Question of the Year, how much I believe life offers far more good then bad. But, I would be a fool to deny that bad things never happen. We know they do. Yet, we also know that people are able to rise above these things and achieve success. Most of us have known someone who, after failing at one thing, went on to succeed at another.

# Failure

"We are all failures – at least, all the best of us are." J. M. Barrie (1860-1937), British playwright. Rectorial address, 3 May 1922, St. Andrew's University, Scotland. Copyright ©1993 by Columbia University Press.

The self-professed Gurus who claim they can free you of fear, bad thoughts and mistakes are wrong. They are also wrong to tell us we can avoid failing or being tempted by bad thoughts and things. According to the early philosophers, the people who promise these things are false prophets. It is the developing and exercising of our character, which allows us to be successful in spite of the uncomfortable obstacles life sometimes presents us.

As you continue your journey toward happier, more loving and successful relationships, remember, you are not perfect. You never will be. When you become afraid, or have bad thoughts, you are simply being human and very normal.

It is only when you allow yourself to act on bad thoughts or to act in disreputable ways that you are acting like a failure. I want to underscore the word acting because you can stop the way you are acting and choose to act differently.

Please take what I have offered as guidance – not as the final word of a Guru. I have stumbled too many times to count and I continue to discover how little I really know. While others have said wonderful things about me and some not so wonderful, I am just a people.

So much of what I do know, I have learned from two primary sources: the people I have had the privilege to work with – some successfully and some not so, and from the mistakes of my own life. While my mistakes have sometimes caused me pain, they have always helped to point me in a better direction.

Someone who has known me a long time said to me, "You should be proud of yourself. You have come a thousand miles over the years." I can still hear my reply: "Thank you for that. Yes, I am proud of what I have accomplished. I also know the thousand miles I have come was only a one hundred-mile trip. I took so many wrong turns in getting here and I still have so far to go."

Thank you for allowing me to act as your host and your guest during this journey. I am interested in what you think and any questions you may have. While I may meet some of you at a seminar or a lecture, I will not meet most of you. Yet, in a metaphoric way, I have met nearly all of you.

During my years of working with couples and individuals, I have been given a true education. I started out knowing so much and after nearly thirty-years in my practice, arrived at knowing how little I know. It is the people I have had the privilege of working with, who have provided me with this education. These hundreds of people represent all of us. This is why I can say I have met nearly all of you.

Again, I thank you for the privilege of being your guide, host and guest for this journey. It is my most fervent wish that your journey continues and that you will go further than I have ever imagined. If you have learned things which will add to your life, I am pleased. It means I have succeeded as your guide.

# Epilogue

Following is an excerpt of an article by Ann Landers. She titled it "Out of the Mouths of Babes." It is about a third grade class project, called "Advice for a Happy Marriage." Here is what the kids said:

1. If someone wants to use something of the other person's, let them use it. Don't let it become a fight.
2. You should have two kids. Four is too many.
3. Take turns doing the chores.
4. I recommend that when you get into a fight, end it being friends.
5. Take the smallest cookie.
6. Go places together, like go out to dinner.
7. Mostly say yes. But if you see you are going to have hot dogs for dinner and you really don't like hot dogs, it is OK to say so.
8. Try not to get a divorce.
9. Be wealthy.
10. Stay lovers for the rest of your lives.
11. Do not marry another person.
12. Take breaks from each other once in a while.
13. If there are two cupcakes and the man takes the one with not as much frosting, he loves you.
14. You need to kiss every once in a while.
15. Sleep together.
16. Have a lot of fun.

The above *suggestions* are probably the best Points to Remember in this book.

# Index

Aaudrillard, Jean, 150
Abuse, 11, 22, 31, 37, 46, 47, 52, 63, 65, 91, 92, 180
Addictive Behavior, 58
Affirmations, 167-169, 176
Alcoholics, 70
Amiel, Henri-frĕdĕric, 229
Anger, 21, 37, 47, 57, 58, 61, 77, 83, 95, 129, 132, 162, 179, 181, 182, 209, 242
Anxiety, 27, 50, 57, 58, 73, 90, 103, 105, 108, 109, 112, 154
Anxiety Factor, 108, 109
Avoidance, 46, 50, 93, 98, 131
Bad Habits, 105, 221
Bad Talking, 178
Bagehot, Walter, 196
Banking the Positives, 148
Barney, Natalie Clifford, 82
Barrie, J.M., 248
Be More Cheerful, 172, 173
Belief System, 50
Berlioz, Hector, 161
Best Wart, 242-244
Big Lie, 14
Blackboard Technique, 53, 166, 170-172, 175, 176, 208, 242
Blamer, 179, 180, 182, 185, 188, 198, 202
Brittain, Vera, 204
Bully, 65, 66, 68
Butler, Samuel, 17
Cannon in D, 170
Cartoon, 96, 171
Cathy, 26-28
Cervantes, 11
Chamberlain, Nevil, 182
Chaos, 15, 23, 31, 46, 61, 77, 92, 100, 110, 121, 218

Chaotic, 21, 23, 25, 48, 51, 58, 76, 100, 125, 152, 183, 207
Character, 117, 221, 225, 227, 228, 235-240, 245, 248
Communication, 31, 34, 42, 46, 52, 53, 61, 90, 92, 162, 164, 178-182, 186, 188-191, 195, 197, 200, 201, 203, 208, 237, 238
Compass Directions, 216
Compromise, 118, 129, 130, 133, 134
Computer, 74, 183-185, 188, 195, 202
Conditioned Reflexes, 175
Conflict Avoidance, 131
Consequence, 198, 199
Core Issues, 36, 40
Counter-beliefs, 170
Crises Factor, 90
Crutch, 56-58, 60, 64, 68, 72, 217
Crutchie, 56-58, 60, 63, 68, 72, 217
Definition of DRS, 31
Denial, 46, 55, 61, 93, 98, 129
Depression, 49, 57-59, 72, 77, 104, 105, 194, 218
Desired Results, 118, 190, 191
Dishonesty, 245
Distracter, 182-185, 188, 198, 202
Distrust, 91
Divorce Statistics, 13
Dog Poo, 157, 158
Domestic Violence, 13
Don and Beth, 130, 131, 134, 136
Dream Car, 154, 155
DRS: Scale Two, 113-116, 120-124
Duc de La Rochefoucauld, 55

Duties, 12, 236
Emerson, Ralph Waldo, 223
Engels, Friedrich, 214
Epictetus, 206
Fade Out, 172
Failure, 13, 48, 104, 167, 170, 206-208, 213, 247, 248
False Prophet, 247
Fast on the Draw, 99, 112, 217
FB, 217-222
Fear, 34, 41-43, 47, 48, 61, 65, 77, 81, 104, 154, 156, 180, 182-184, 219, 247, 248
Fear of Rejection, 42, 156
Feedback, 230
Feelings, 11, 27, 47, 82-88, 99, 105, 110, 189, 191-194, 203, 213, 219, 224, 231, 232
Flash Cards, 53, 165, 169, 172-176, 208, 242
Flirt, 74, 224
Foundation Issues, 36
Four Steps Communication, 162, 178, 189, 191, 195, 197, 200, 201, 203, 208, 238
Fulgum, Robert, 165
Furious, 194, 197
Gambling, 221
Generic Feelings, 193
Gottman, John, 144, 145
Gratitude, 57, 145, 146, 149
Greek Tragedy, 177
Guru, 246, 248
Gypsy Fortune Telling, 224
Hallucinations, 86, 87
Hammarskjöld, Dag, 237
Heller, Steve, 51, 216
Helpless, 43, 44, 66
Herb and Sylvia, 94
Hewison, Robert, 18
Hobbes, Thomas, 22
Information:, 150
Insane, 69-72, 190

Insanity, 28, 69, 70, 72, 74, 80, 84, 88, 89, 96, 187, 203, 207
Instant Attraction, 83-89, 207
Instant Love, 81, 87, 89
Instant Relationships, 13
Inventory, 86, 161
James, William, 153
Jerk, 77, 78
Jerome, Jerome K., 142
Jim and the Damsel, 71
Johnson, Samuel, 208
Joke, 126, 128
Justification, 91
Keats, John, 83
Keeping Score, 119
Landers, Ann, 250
Levenson, Robert, 144, 145
Life Plan, 128
Linda and the Jerk, 77
Little Ones, 201
Lone Ranger, 72
Lord Acton, 200
Lord Chesterfield, 246
Lost Soul, 58-60, 63, 68
Louise Bewitched, 102-104
Love at First Sight, 39, 43, 82-84, 86-88
Map Making, 137, 205, 208, 211, 217, 230
Marital Problems, 122
Massie, Allan, 226
Mean-spirited, 199
Metaphor, 50, 59, 60, 180, 211, 243, 246, 247
Misstatements, 245
Money Issues, 127
Monsters and Magical Sticks, 216
Most Important Question, 15, 34, 125, 126, 134, 138
Mr. Right, 26, 27, 38
Mutual Attraction, 82, 131
Neatness Freak, 232, 233
Negative Influences, 142, 143

## Index    253

Negative People, 106
Negativity, 106-108, 112, 159, 162
New Maps, 208
Obligations, 12, 220, 225-228, 230, 236-238, 241
Obsessing, 27, 101-104, 109, 112
Opinions, 118, 157, 184, 192, 203, 230
Otis Factor, 109, 110
Pachelbel, 170
Paglia, Camille, 212
Pander, 153
Panic Attacks, 103
Parent/Child, 62
Partnership, 12, 13
Past:, 18
Patient, 16, 39, 60, 61, 63, 68, 123, 163, 217
Paula and Alan, 121
Perceived Levels, 155
Perfection, 168
Photographs, 135
Placater, 181, 182, 188, 202
Pleasure List, 146
Poe, Edgar Allan, 185
Positive Activities, 143
Positive Aspects, 107, 143, 144, 147-149, 160, 162
Positive Attributes, 76
Positive Factors, 144, 145, 148
Pupil, 62, 63, 68
Quarters, 157, 158
Question of the Year, 102, 139-143, 149, 208, 219, 247
Quixote, 11
Rabbi, 66, 244, 245
Rage, 47, 57, 65, 66, 179
Reagan, Ronald, 227
Rebound, 64, 68, 75, 217
Recurring Insanity, 72
Recurring Patterns, 91
Rejection, 42, 43, 49, 156

Relationship Strategy, 162
Religion, 33, 125, 128, 137
Resentment, 57, 58, 132, 180, 209, 231
Resolution, 191, 192, 197-199, 203
Restoration, 120
Robert and Betty, 32, 35, 37, 38
Sad Sack, 63, 68
Sally, 114, 115
Salter, Andrew, 175, 176
Santayana, George, 225
Satir, Virginia, 178, 179, 181, 188, 191
Savior, 58, 59, 64, 68
School Days, 165
Sculpting, 229
Seeking Levels, 155
Self-absorbed, 217-219, 228
Self-destructive, 45
Self-doubt, 45, 48
Self-Esteem, 45, 51, 100, 152-157, 159, 161, 164, 165, 168, 227, 228
Self-Evaluation, 32, 91, 93, 94, 96-98, 155
Self-Fulfilling Prophecy, 49-52, 54, 157, 158, 166
Self-hate, 45, 48
Self-hypnosis, 170, 242
Sexual Intimacy, 132, 211, 212
Sexual Relationships, 95
Sisyphus, 177
Slob, 231-234
Smothering, 45
Storr, Anthony, 102
Straight Talk, 186
Sylvia, 94-96, 146, 147
Targeted Belief, 170, 172
Teacher, 62-64, 68, 161, 244, 247
Ten Factors, 13
Therapist, 9, 12, 60, 61, 64, 68, 122, 186, 193, 200
Three for One, 52, 53, 159, 160, 162-164, 208

Top Dog, 67
Twelve Patterns, 89, 90, 92, 96, 98, 110
Twelve Steps, 213
Unconscious Processes, 85
Unrealistic Expectations, 217, 219, 240
Van Buren, Abigail, 227
Victim, 44, 47, 65, 66, 68, 78, 181
Violence, 13, 37, 45-47, 52, 180
Warning, 13-15, 20, 43, 77, 78, 84, 88, 89, 102, 108, 198
Watzlawick, Paul, 153, 206
Webster, John, 205
Wellness Letter, 143
Whitman, Walt, 139
Withdrawal Symptoms, 104-106
Wylie, Elinor, 130

## *When Cupid's Arrow is a Pain in the Ass*
### ORDER FORM OR SEMINAR INFORMATION

By Mail: **H.I. Enterprises**
**P.O. Box 3604**
**Thousand Oaks, CA 91359-0604**
Check, Money Order or Credit Card Orders

By Phone: **(800) 806-0407** USA
Credit Card Orders Only

By Fax: **(818) 865-0818**
Credit Card Orders Only

Price per Book: $12.95
Shipping & Handling (USA Rates): $2.25 (First Book)
$1.00 (Each Additional)

Sales Tax: California Residents add $.94

☐ I would like information on your seminars.

**Payment Method:**
☐ Check or Money Order (Payable to H.I. Enterprises)
☐ Master Card    ☐ VISA    ☐ A/E    ☐ Discover

**Name:**_____

**Street:**_____

**City:**_____

**State:**_____ **Zip Code:**_____

**Telephone: (      )**_____

**Name on Credit Card:**_____
**Credit Card Number:** _____
**Exp. Date:** _____

I understand that I may return this book for a full refund – for any reason – no questions asked.